ENDORSEMENTS

Signs of a coming revival seem to be appearing all around us. Tom Phillips shares some extraordinary insights and encouragement in this "cutting edge" book. Every Christian will be both blessed and challenged by reading it and responding to its message.

—PAUL A. CEDAR
President, Mission America Coalition

At a time when all the tabloids, talk shows, and enemies in high places are slandering our Lord and the gospel, God has been working quietly to undermine their strategies and revive His work. At this very moment, there is a mighty move of God mushrooming to unprecedented levels, eclipsing everything to the contrary. A spirit of anticipation is everywhere.

—DANNY DE LEON
Pastor, Templo Calvario Church, Santa Ana, CA

America's spiritual history has included significant tides of spiritual awakening that influenced entire generations for Christ. Over and over again, God has rescued us when we have united together in prayer. Following the low spiritual tide of the last few decades, America is once again poised to see an inrushing of God's presence that will drive away darkness and despair. Dr. Phillips' new book, *Jesus Now*, charts a course for your involvement in this new awakening. Together we can see America's spiritual tide rise again!

—DR. WILLIAM M. WILSON
President, Oral Roberts University

"The Kingdom of God is not going to arrive on Air Force One," said Chuck Colson. Politicians are not going to save America. Wall Street is not going to save America. If America is to be saved, Tom Phillips' new book, *Jesus Now*, points to the cure: Jesus. *Jesus Now* reinforces Fyodor Dostoevsky's insight, "The West has lost Christ, and that is why it is dying; that is the only reason."

—DAVID LANE
American Renewal Project

Perhaps one of the most important aspects of revival is hope—the hope that God is not done with us yet and is preparing to do a new thing in our midst. Tom Phillips gives us that hope powerfully in his new book, *Jesus Now*. Your prayers for revival will arise on fresh wings of hope after reading this book.

—DR. DAVID BUTTS, CHAIRMAN
America's National Prayer Committee

In a nation that has its share of bad news, *Jesus Now* is like a refreshing breeze of hope. Tom Phillips' passion for revival and awakening will not only inspire you to believe but challenge you to become engaged in this next great move of God in America.

—KAY HORNER
Executive Director, Awakening America Alliance

The title of this book says it all and echoes the hearts of Christians all across this nation: we need *Jesus now*! In this book, Tom Phillips shows how sparks of revival are already beginning to ignite inside the church, which is our only hope for restoration in America. The principles of God's Word energized by the power of the Holy Spirit in revived hearts will usher in the greatest revival our nation has ever seen. Our country will then be the key servant-leader God intended it to be, promoting truth, justice, compassion, and love. We enthusiastically endorse *Jesus Now*.

—DAVID AND JASON BENHAM
authors of *Whatever the Cost* and *Living Among Lions*,
benhambrothers.com

Do you aspire to be a part of the next great movement of God in our generation? If so, read Tom Phillips' newest book, *Jesus Now*, which will inspire you to go deeper with God than ever before. The greatest need in America today is the next Great Awakening! The seeds sown through the pages of this book could potentially lead you into a day of fruitfulness unprecedented in your life. Read it and share it with a friend.

—DR. RONNIE FLOYD
Senior Pastor, Cross Church, and past President,
Southern Baptist Convention

I have grave concerns that are addressed so well by my friend, Tom Phillips, in his book *Jesus Now*. When people's hearts are awakened, then they will know the value of religious faith and freedom. I highly endorse this book.

—FRANK WOLF
former Congressman (Ret. 1981–2014)

In today's world, many people feel discouraged, fearful, and oppressed. In *Jesus Now*, this powerful book full of revelation, Tom Phillips inspires Christ-followers to have *hope*. Countless believers today cry out to the Lord, "Will you not revive us again, that your people may rejoice in you" (Psalm 85:6 ESV)? Tom Phillips is one of the most knowledgeable leaders on the topics of revival and renewal that we have in today's church. *Jesus*

Now describes the moving of the Holy Spirit in a believer's life throughout America and the world. When reading this helpful book, I felt a sense of excitement, anticipation, and revival. I didn't want to stop reading—rejoicing all the way!

—WAYDE GOODALL
Dean of College Ministry, Professor of Church Leadership,
Director of Graduate Programs,
and President of Worldwide Family at Northwest University

Dr. Tom Phillips has been at the forefront of Christian service for decades. In his latest book, *Jesus Now*, he writes with insight, wisdom, and a remarkable understanding of God at work in the church today. If you are seeking to be refreshed and renewed by God's purposeful initiative in the past and how He continues to work in remarkable ways through the seemingly insignificant and the ordinary, then *Jesus Now* is for you. But be careful: engaging with God at this level may just change who you are and take you to a deeper relationship with Him.

—REV. DR. RICHARD GIBBONS
Senior Pastor at First Presbyterian Church,
Greenville, South Carolina

Tom Phillips loves Jesus and he loves people. Moreover, he has a great yearning for revival. Reading this book will stir your heart and prod you to believe God for greater things.

—DR. ROBERT E. COLEMAN

Tom Phillips has been a friend and a collaborator of mine in evangelism and revival for over twenty-five years. *Jesus Now* is his mirror image. It combines his voice as a messenger of hope with his intense desire to see people and cultures transformed by the power of Jesus Christ. For Tom, God's glorious work today presages an historic work—soon to come, I'm convinced. *Jesus Now* is infectious. It will focus your priorities, intensify your hunger, and inspire you with confidence.

—DR. BOB BAKKE
Teaching Pastor at Hillside Church of Bloomington
and member of OneCry in Buchanan, Michigan

Jesus Now is timely and dynamic and moved my heart deeply. Hunger and thirst for personal and corporate revival drips from every page and echoes the heart cry of so many who are interceding for revival in the church today. *Jesus Now* should be put in the hands of every church leader in North America.

—JEFF FARMER
President of Pentecostal/Charismatic Churches of North America

Prepare to be inspired and ignited! In his book *Jesus Now*, Dr. Tom Phillips turns our attention to Jesus' loving pursuit of us in everyday events we may be missing. People of all generations, color, and backgrounds are responding to Christ's powerful transformation of their lives with passionate prayer, sacrificial care, and a bold sharing of the gospel. This book shakes us from distraction, disillusionment, and spiritual dozing to the powerful plan that Jesus is awakening His church to reset and revive us to complete the Great Commission.

—KATHY BRANZELL
National Coordinator of LOVE2020

Jesus Now is an extraordinary book—a must-read for all believers who are holding onto hope for awakening in America. Tom's ability to weave engaging stories, revival history, and practical principles is sheer genius. In times when ordinary has become the norm, *Jesus Now* awakens readers to the attainability of living a fruitful Christian life. We are on the brink of an outpouring in our nation, and it is an honor to be a part of this Jesus Now Awakening.

—COREY LEE
Pastor of Convergence Church

Tom Phillips is a champion for revival and renewal efforts. His unique perspective, having worked with the Billy Graham organization for decades, has afforded him a rare window on God's activity in the world. His book is filled with the principles that drive revival and is readable and compelling. It offers a lens through which we better discern God's work, not only in history but in our times.

—P. DOUGLAS SMALL
President of Project Pray

Having given his life to the cause of revival throughout the world through his work with the Billy Graham Evangelistic Association, Tom Phillips powerfully calls the church in America to a time of increased sensitivity and responsiveness to the ways in which God is currently working. It is a *Jesus Now* time.

—CLAUDE ALEXANDER
Pastor of The Park Church in Charlotte, North Carolina

Tom Phillips warmly and transparently invites us to seek Jesus for how *we* might be involved in burgeoning reawakening with *Jesus Now*—from a personal level of revival to a corporate level of spiritual outpouring—offering "Spirit Empowered Faith" lessons along the way to guide the reader into a deeper relationship with Jesus and a greater understanding of his or her role in revival. And we *all* can have a role!

—DONICA HUDSON
founder and President of In His Presence Global Ministries, Inc., revivalist, and host of Charlotte Alive, YouTube Channel, YouTube.com/user/CharlotteAlive

In two simple but profound words, Tom has captured the heart and hope of God for our day—*Jesus Now!* Today's fresh stirrings of awakening as captured in this timely work are all about intimacy with the historical and contemporary person of Jesus. And it's the urgency of *now* that makes our pleadings for awakening personal and practical as illustrated in the powerful stories Tom has chronicled for us. Read it and reap great blessings as the Spirit enlists your heart into all He is up to in our day.

—DR. DAVID FERGUSON
Great Commandment Network

I agree with Tom Phillips. God is indeed moving today. In so many places, people are responding to Him. We should be encouraged and ask God how we can be involved.

—DR. STEVE DOUGLASS
President of Cru

I've had the privilege of knowing Dr. Phillips for many years, partnered in ministry with him, and served on various boards together. His passion for God and for revival is consistent and unwavering. Tom's book, *Jesus Now*, is an amazing resource born out of a lifetime of his personal hunger, study, experiences, and contending for the authentic. *Jesus Now* not only inspires us through what God has done in past revivals, but also equips us with practical understanding of their commonalities and potential hindrances. This is a much-needed book with a timely message by a man who truly understands what it will take to see a great awakening and mighty harvest.

—DR. DOUG STRINGER
Founder and President, Somebody Cares America and
Somebody Cares International, Houston, Texas

JESUS NOW

God Is Up to Something Big

Tom Phillips

BroadStreet
PUBLISHING

BroadStreet Publishing Group, LLC
Racine, Wisconsin, USA
BroadStreetPublishing.com

JESUS NOW God Is Up to Something Big

Stock or custom editions of BroadStreet Publishing titles may be purchased in
bulk for educational, business, ministry, fundraising, or sales promotional use. For
information, please e-mail info@broadstreetpublishing.com.

Cover design by Chris Garborg, GarborgDesign.com
Interior design and typeset by Katherine Lloyd, theDESKonline.com

Printed in the United States of America
16 17 18 19 20 5 4 3 2 1

To Ouida,
my partner in the greatest life a man could have.
Thanks, honey, for the consistent encouragement
to write this book and for the support during it.

CONTENTS

FOREWORD

s America in the early stages of a spiritual revival, which will overshadow anything we have ever seen before in our nation's history?

Tom Phillips makes a convincing case that this could be true, as he examines some of the significant new ways God is at work touching lives today. Only history will be able to tell us if his thesis is accurate, for we are too near to these events to judge—but no one can read this book and not be touched by the way God is working today in the lives of countless men and women who formerly gave little thought to Christ.

For many years, Tom Phillips has been a valued member of our team, and I know of few individuals who have a deeper commitment to evangelism and a broader understanding of what is happening spiritually across our land. His book is a vivid and compelling testimony to the truth that the gospel in all of its fullness is still (in Paul's words) "the power of God for the salvation of everyone who believes." As he recounts, Tom has experienced that truth in his own life, and I believe every reader of his book will experience it too as they open their hearts to the molding and life-changing power of Jesus Christ.

—Billy Graham
Charlotte, North Carolina
(written for *Revival Signs*, upon which *Jesus Now!* is based)

PREFACE

Look among the nations, and see;
wonder and be astounded.
For I am doing a work in your days
that you would not believe if told.
—Habakkuk 1:5 ESV

Not long ago, I went to a local garden center with my wife, Ouida. I needed some help. I couldn't get anything to grow. When I told this to one of the garden center staff, he said, "You need peppermint!"

"Peppermint?"

"Once it gets going," he said, "there's no stopping it. Besides, it's beautiful."

"Don't do it," Ouida whispered to me. What did she know that I didn't?

I debated carefully a few seconds and then said, "Sold" to the garden guy. As we walked back to the car with a handful of peppermint plants, Ouida said to me, "You're going to have to control it."

"Yes, dear."

Once back home, I got down on my knees in the dirt. The sweet scent of peppermint was unbelievable. The directions said: "Plant in moist soil. Full sun preferred. Don't overwater." I dug some small holes and nestled each peppermint plant in the ground. Then I gave each of them some water, stood up, and wiped the dirt from my knees.

Every day, I came outside and looked at my tiny plants. Soon, they weren't so little. Maybe my wife was right after all. Once it takes root, nothing can stop peppermint from growing and spreading.

Could the aroma of peppermint be a living metaphor for the undeniably sweet scent of a gracious Father, redeeming Son, and the fresh empowering Holy Spirit now spreading throughout our land? What if I told you there is a fresh, sweet Spirit of God now growing and spreading throughout churches, neighborhoods, businesses, and schools in our country? What if our prayer for Jesus to revive hearts and renew our land is happening now? This resource is to encourage you and me to join Jesus in what He is already doing. Read just a few examples of what Jesus is doing now:

- A courageous teacher taught her public school, eighth-grade class by introducing them to revered ancient wisdom literature—known as the book of Proverbs
- A former top executive for Apple leveraged his passion for technology into a portal for online evangelism involving 9,000 missionaries in 129 countries, reaching 400 million people daily
- A college student-turned-preacher from North Dakota is at the forefront of an emerging movement among hundreds of thousands of millennials engaging, loving, and serving Jesus through a simple, startling six-word prayer
- A prayer and worship group of older men became young at heart through an influx of teens with a deepening desire to learn intercessory prayer
- A pastor who sought the Lord to reign over his community and who, in the aftermath of a devastating

tornado, was invited, out of the blue, by state and county officials to direct the local disaster relief effort—which propelled local churches to new unity in serving the physical, emotional, and spiritual needs of their hurting neighbors in the name of Jesus

- A wife and mother in South Carolina who found herself face-to-face with the governor of her state invited her state's highest official to pray together—right then and there
- An East Coast businessman's life was turned upsidedown as he turned from self-determination and began to lay every care, concern, desire, and need on the altar and into the hands of Jesus Christ
- A woman whose persevering faith and commitment to prayer has been a catalyst for growing numbers of Christian believers and seekers alike in Hollywood to turn to Jesus

As you read these stories, recall the words of the prophet Ezekiel: "I will accept you as fragrant incense when I bring you out from the nations and gather you from the countries where you have been scattered, and I will be proved holy through you in the sight of the nations" (Ezekiel 20:41 NIV).

In Jesus and through the promised Holy Spirit, a new day of spiritual awakening, fresh as the scent of peppermint, is upon us. "For we are to God the fragrance of Christ among those who are being saved and among those who are perishing. To the one we are the aroma of death leading to death, and to the other the aroma of life leading to life. And who is sufficient for these things? For we are not, as so many, peddling the word of God; but as of sincerity, but as from God, we speak in the sight of God in Christ" (2 Corinthians 2:15–17).

The word has already begun to spread: the sweet scent of revival is in the air. Because of Jesus, our churches, our nation, our lives may never be the same again. Stay with me on this journey, and you'll catch the passion and possibilities of Jesus now!

Revival—One Life at a Time

G od is intent on bringing His people to Himself. Why should this profound truth matter? It should matter because we are living in an extraordinary moment when God is awakening the church through the reconciling love of the Son, Jesus, and the power of the Holy Spirit.

Only a few times in history has our nation experienced such a "Jesus-Now Awakening."

What if the Lord was already awakening you, your family, your church, your city? Are you open to the chance that God's Spirit, without warning, could sweep through your own life? I dearly hope so. That's why I wrote this book, to encourage and nurture such a hope.

It's a hope I've cherished for a long time. The seed of it was planted when I was a small child, on a country drive near Corinth, Mississippi, where I grew up. I can still see the tiny shacks from the car window and hear myself asking my mother, "Why do the black people live there, Mom?"

"That's just the way it is, son." I wept.

Since that country ride with my mother, my increasing understanding of God's gloriously planned variety of color in people and His wish for our unequivocal acceptance of each other has grown. I sensed then, as I now am certain, that if spiritual awakening is real, then the refreshing winds of the Spirit will touch not just the people in the church pews but also the most remote, insensitive hearts and the many shades of prejudice and hate that segregate us from each other and from God.

Fast-forward twenty years to a small church near the town of Water Valley, Mississippi. Whenever I would come home from college on a short break or for the summer, I would drop off Ouida at our house and then visit "my parish." I visited each home with the white people and black people, everyone. God had put them there. They were His people, and I loved them in the name of Jesus.

That was when the church deacons pulled me aside and said, "Tom, we need to talk to you about your visitation."

"Why?"

"You're visiting black people."

"Sure," I said. "They're no different from any of us. They live here. They're people. God created them. They're part His family."

The deacons just looked at me until one of them said, "Well, this is a white church, and you can't do this."

That next Sunday I preached about love, the love of Jesus that embraces all people, all of God's children—"God is love" (1 John 4:8). I made it clear that anyone coming into the sanctuary would not be stopped, but be welcomed. After the service, I was standing at the front door greeting the people as they left. One deacon, a white gentleman, said to me, "I know what point you were trying to make, but I still love you anyway."

Yet, something else happened. I noticed that younger people seemed to appreciate the sermon. In fact, the younger the person the more he or she said, "The things you said about Jesus loving *all* people, regardless of race, are real. It's what God says."

That day, I began to see the differing perspectives of the older and younger generations. The former tended to have remote, insensitive, fearful hearts. Young people, on the other hand, were more open to following the Holy Spirit and the Word of God.

How willing are you? How willing am I to do the same? My hunger for personal revival and spiritual awakening across our land is as strong as my desire to be used in the reconciliation between blacks and whites, all peoples. I wrote it down on a yellow pad list, "The Fourteen Things I Hope to Accomplish Before I Die." I have seen African-American and Asian pastors from Philadelphia confess to each other their racism and then break down weeping. I've seen pride broken, sins confessed, and lives restored in the most calloused hearts and in the most unlikely parts of the country. I believe these and other acts of reconciliation and healing are God's notes on *His* yellow pad—to give us a peek at the present, unfolding revival.

WHERE'S JESUS NOW?

Is a fresh revival ready to sweep across this nation? Is it already happening? Could God really be about to ignite a holy fire that could kindle the hearts of millions with a holy passion for Himself and His kingdom? While I believe the answer is yes, I know one thing for sure: God sees beyond our crippling human condition to the new life in Christ He desires for every person.

I remember when the wife of a pro-basketball player told her story on the final day of a Billy Graham Crusade in San Diego. She was divorced and hurting. She turned to drugs and became one of Satan's prized examples of how people build their own prison with chemicals—until Christ set her free. She described how others could also find the freedom she now enjoyed.

After the San Diego crusade, I received a one-page letter with these three lines:

Me full of heroin.

Pockets full of heroin.

And I went forward to receive Jesus.

The letter was signed by Raul Gonzales, who was in the audience that day. He had been a drug addict living on a diet of pills and powder until his self-punishment became too great. After he met Christ, he returned to the people who had managed to survive his real-life nightmare. Raul became a part of the Jesus-Now Awakening, and for over twenty years, he and his group (Teen Challenge, in Hartford, Connecticut) have led pimps and pushers to a Carpenter from Nazareth who has helped them rebuild their lives. "We are seeing revival in our cities," says Raul. "It is happening with people who have nothing but Christ."[1]

Should I have been surprised that one as humble as Raul is actually a crack of light, part of a new spiritual awakening?

Should I have been surprised that God works through the weak, the poor, and the unlikely?

People ask me, "What does revival look like? Will we know it when we see it? What if revival were happening right now?"

What if you and I could be a part of this Jesus-Now Awakening? I wonder what God could do if we *all* found our place in this new spiritual awakening?

Recently, a man came to my office at the Billy Graham Library. People I greatly trust had told me, "You've got to meet this guy." Bruce Snell played briefly in the NFL before going into business. Out of his growing thirst for Jesus, he was leading a series of prayer meetings. After a friendly greeting, Bruce looked at me and said, "Everywhere I go, to churches and prayer gatherings throughout South Carolina and North Carolina, I keep running into personal revival."

The power of God soon filled the room. A gentleman, named Wayne, and I waited, attentive to the Spirit. We were ready to go to prayer when Bruce said, "The Lord is telling me to anoint you, Tom, and you, Wayne. Do either of you have oil I can use to anoint you both?"

"I do," Wayne said. "I got it just two weeks ago."

Our prayers lasted two hours. We were on our knees, lifting up the Lord, praising the Lord, seeking the Lord for His church, His children, His world. We prayed for the Holy Spirit to wash over us. The Lord's presence was undeniable.

Our prayer time ended, and we stood up to leave. I stayed in my office, while Bruce and Wayne turned to go out to the parking lot. Not long after, Bruce called to thank me for our visit. I'm glad I was sitting down.

"Tom, this may sound crazy to you, but as Wayne and I were walking out of the building, it looked like Wayne was walking above the ground." Bruce wasn't finished talking. "Wayne just called. He said he was so overwhelmed in the Spirit. I said nothing to him about how I saw him walking as if floating. Wayne said, 'Bruce, as we left Tom's office, I felt like I was walking on air.'"

Continuing, Bruce said: "Recently, I was working in the yard and wanting to put in some new plants. My wife, Karen, said to me, 'Whatever you do, don't plant peppermint. It will take over the garden.' I said, 'Fine, I'll plant it in the large pot.' A few days later, I was talking to a friend who said he and his wife had a similar conversation about the uncontainable, untamed nature of peppermint."

What if God is already spreading the gladness of His unmistakable, refreshing Holy Spirit throughout our land? I believe that's exactly what He's doing. Throughout the US, patches of peppermint are growing in cultures where the God of Abraham, Isaac, and Jacob is scorned. In countries bereft and barren of the fruit of the Holy Spirit, where darkening confusion, bitterness, and strife are growing—countries like the United States of America!—a new ripening season, a new life-giving harvest, rooted in Jesus is upon us.

I wasn't quite as eager to receive Bruce's next words.

"Tom, the Lord told me that His followers, His body, the church, are ripe for deception."

"What do you mean?" I asked.

"Tom, it's as if Jesus said to me: 'My people want the things of the Lord. They want the things I have to give, but do you want *me*? Do you believe that I AM?

You want peace. *I am* peace.

You want hope. *I am* hope,

You want forgiveness. *I am* forgiveness.

You want reconciliation. *I am* reconciliation.

You want healing. *I am* healing.

You want new life. *I am* new life.

You want love. *I am* love.

Don't let your pursuit of ministry replace the relationship, the salvation, the hope and the new life in me.'"

Can you hear, can you see, can you savor the unconditional, uncontainable love of Jesus in these words? You are not alone. You are like Bruce Snell and others in big cities, small towns, and remote parts across our land, a people of gladness—the gladness of the Lord. Who are some of these people? What can they reveal to us and teach us about the Jesus-Now Awakening that is spreading but yet a sprout; that is fully present and yet budding with potential; that is now and not yet?

There are no words to describe the fresh scent of peppermint.

Breathe in the amazing stories that follow and see what might happen as the fresh gladness of God breathes in you, and then ask yourself: "How do I fit into this Jesus-Now Awakening?"

God's spiritual awakening has now begun to dawn. The people you will meet in this book are living proof. These people and many others are coming face-to-face with their undeniable need for a personal relationship with God, who can only be found through Jesus Christ. In people such as these, I see a God who can heal our land in a way that could touch every corner of economic, social, and spiritual need.

This God, who has been at work throughout history to bring people to Himself, is once more making history in our time. From national youth gatherings that attract hundreds to prayer meetings in public high schools to small inner-city churches, the God of the Bible is doing something you and I never could have imagined—until now. So let's join Him!

THE JESUS-NOW AWAKENING

Join the Jesus-Now Awakening as you live out a Spirit-empowered faith. *Jesus Now* is designed to engage followers of Jesus as they impart both the gospel and their life while living out a relevant, daily faith (1 Thessalonians 2:7–8). Just as the Word became flesh and "moved into the neighborhood," through the prompting and power of His Spirit, we can live out a Jesus-Now Awakening in our world (John 1:14 MSG).

Jesus Now is unique. It is unlike any of the resources you've likely read before because the exercises in each chapter were written with the specific goal of engaging you in the Jesus-Now Awakening. These exercises are created to move beyond seeking to simply know or study God's truth and move toward actually experiencing it. Why is this important? It's only an experiential, Spirit-empowered faith that can live out a Jesus-Now Awakening.

You'll be able to identify the experiential exercises in *Jesus Now* in the bracketed boxes of the text. They can be used in a variety of settings such as: personal devotions, mentoring relationships, and small groups.

The *Jesus-Now* resource is designed to foster a Spirit-empowered faith. A framework for spiritual growth has been drawn from a cluster analysis of several Greek and Hebrew words, which declare that Christ's followers are to be equipped for works of ministry or service. Therefore, within the *Jesus-Now* resource, you'll find specific exercises that are designed and organized around four themes. A Spirit-empowered disciple:

- LOVES the LORD (Acts 13:2 NASB) – Exercises designed to strengthen this area of spiritual growth are marked L1–L10.
- LOVES the WORD (Acts 6:4 NASB) – Exercises for building up this aspect of spiritual growth are marked W1– W10.
- LOVES His PEOPLE (Galatians 5:13 NASB) – Exercises intended to equip this area of growth are marked P1– P10.
- LOVES His MISSION (2 Corinthians 5:18 NASB) – Exercises provided to strengthen this area of growth are marked M1– M10.

Imagine this: You've just begun a journey in the *Jesus Now* resource. It's as if you're going for a walk. As you read through *Jesus Now*, we invite you to walk:

- In the light of God's Son—John 8:12
- In the light of God's Word—Psalm 119:105
- In the light of God's people—Matthew 5:14

The bracketed boxes and exercises in them are designed around these three sources of God's light. They'll encourage your awakening journey as a Spirit-empowered disciple of Jesus. We're delighted that you've decided to take this walk with us. God's Word reminds us that it's vitally important to walk in the light.

"Walk while you have the light" (John 12:35).

The Great Commandment Network has developed the experiential exercises, the Spirit-empowered discipleship framework, and in collaboration with others, the Spirit-empowered outcomes that are included in the appendix of this resource (see pages 204-215). The Great Commandment's deepest desire is to serve our friend, Dr. Tom Phillips, and the Jesus-Now Awakening through our contributions.

The Great Commandment Network is an international collaborative network of strategic, kingdom leaders from the faith community, marketplace, education, and caregiving fields who prioritize the powerful simplicity of the words of Jesus to love God, love others, and see others become His followers (Matthew 22:37–40, Matthew 28:19–20).

ONE

Ordinary People Living Quiet, Anonymous Lives, Until ...

At a middle school in North Carolina, eighth-grade teacher Carolyn James[1] was growing restless. She loved her students, yet, after two years on the job, her prayers started to overflow with questions. "Why, Lord," she prayed, "is there no Christian ministry on campus? Why don't I see anyone on campus doing something for the Lord?"

One day, she heard the Lord answer back: "Why not you, Carolyn?"

A short time later, Carolyn began meeting with a friend, and the idea of starting a service-learning club, dedicated to serving others, began to gel. A few days later, the unexpected took place when Sue, another friend of Carolyn's, came to her school, and before the first bell rang, began praying over Carolyn's classroom. As Sue prayed, the image of a vineyard emerged.

"At that moment, I didn't yet realize what a vineyard had to do with my students, but it was clear that there was fruit to be harvested in my classroom. The fruit had to do with growing the intelligence and wisdom of my students, some of whom knew the

Lord and others had no idea there existed a God who loved them unconditionally, both now and eternally, in Jesus Christ."

Carolyn knew the vine of intelligence and wisdom that could take root and spread in the minds and hearts of her students was within arm's reach. She took her Bible, opened it to Proverbs, and said a prayer. Two hours later, she had thirty freshly photocopied editions of "Historic Wisdom." Each contained all thirty-one chapters of Proverbs without the title.

On the first day of class, she gave each student a copy and then said to him or her, "I want you to grow academically through this school year. I want you to grow in intelligence and wisdom, and to that end, I've collected some timeless, historic quotes. Every morning before we start class, you'll have ten to fifteen minutes to warm up your brain. You can choose any page, start reading any chapter."

The students more than went along with the assignment. They took their teacher's invitation to heart. One morning, Carolyn asked if anyone wanted to share a sentence or two. A boy named Curt raised his hand,—"The fear of the Lord is the beginning of wisdom."

Carolyn asked, "What did that mean to you?"

Curt replied, "It just really spoke to me."

One day Carolyn took a photo of her class. She pondered the tiny image on her smart phone, and then it hit her: "I have thirty kids who are seriously reflecting on the Scriptures fifteen minutes a day, Monday through Friday." But there was more wisdom, more opportunity to be had. Brenda told her story to fifteen ninth-grade girls she was mentoring at church. Then she challenged them: "If my students in a public school classroom can read five chapters of Proverbs every week, you can easily do as much."

Carolyn's "history experiment" began to spread throughout

the school. A curious administrator came to her classroom one morning. "He told me that we don't allow religious reading in a public school." His visits became more frequent. Yet, never did he tell Carolyn to put away "Historic Wisdom." Instead, the vineyard she had "planted" kept growing, yet with no apparent harvest.

The Lord's perfect, unpredictable timing took hold. At the beginning of the fourth academic year since her classes had been reading "Historic Wisdom," Carolyn had serious questions. "All along, I wanted to see the fruit of my vineyard. Then, in my daily reading, I came across the words of Leviticus: 'When you come into the land and plant any kind of tree for food, regard its fruit as forbidden. For three years you are to consider it forbidden; it must not be eaten. In the fourth year all its fruit will be holy, an offering of praise to the LORD. But in the fifth year you may eat of its fruits. In this way your harvest will be increased. I am the LORD your God' (Leviticus19:23-25 NIV).

"I had been trying to figure out how to reap a harvest on my own. I stopped and said, 'Lord, where is *your* harvest?'"

That fall, Carolyn befriended Jill, a new eighth-grade teacher, and invited her to church. A short time later, through the course of their conversation, Carolyn's prayers, and God's faithfulness, Jill gave her life to Jesus Christ.

"The Lord said to me, 'If you can win your co-workers to me, you can certainly influence your students,'" Carolyn commented.

Carolyn's story is but a peek at how God is stirring across our land.

If it had been just an isolated incident or two, I may have discarded the events of the past ten years in a file marked "coincidence." However, as more and more stories like Carolyn's have surfaced, the remarkable movement of God is now impossible to ignore.

Walking in the Light of God's Word

Your word is a lamp to my feet and a light to my path.
(Psalm 119:105, ESV)

Pause to consider how you too could awaken others to the transforming power of God's Word. Try this: Begin a spiritual conversation about your renewed gratitude for God's Word. Your conversations might sound like:

- *I have a new appreciation for how God's Word can "work" in our lives. I've recently seen how the Bible can ...*
- *I've never really understood how the Bible can make a difference in things today, but I can now see ...*
- *I am so glad that God gave us the Bible. It's been like a blueprint—a set of plans or instructions for how to do life. I'm grateful for those plans because they've helped me.*

Pray with a partner or small group, asking God to bring to mind specific Bible verses that you have lived out. Next, ask the Holy Spirit to empower you to share His Word with others.

W-4 Humbly and vulnerably sharing of the Spirit's transforming work through the Word

SPIRIT-EMPOWERED *Faith*

At a small downtown community church in Memphis, Tennessee, thirty-five men gathered for a special Saturday morning meeting. They had learned that Bill, a man in their congregation, whose marriage was now crumbling, had been seeing another woman. Opinion in the room ranged from judgment to confusion. As the pastor prepared to start the discussion, the agenda hit a snag. Bill stood up. His voice began to break, and he began to weep.

"I have done everything I can to restore my marriage, but it hasn't worked. I hope none of you ever have to go through what I've experienced in the past couple of years."

Before the morning was over, twenty other men spoke up and confessed their own struggles. Weeks later, these same men started a monthly gathering to pray for the church and each other. It was the first time such a thing had taken place in the church's short, eighteen-year history.

In Portland, Oregon, the pastor of a large church attended an inaugural prayer summit with forty-five other pastors from the Portland area. As he sat in the evening communion service, he was privately skeptical about what could really happen between a group of pastors from different denominations. As a Pentecostal, he was aware of the lingering animosity between his denomination and some of the area's Conservative Baptists.

After communion, a fellow pastor, whom he did not know, came to the communion table and addressed the group. "I want to confess, tonight, that I stand here as a part of the Conservative Baptists in Portland, and I ask forgiveness of my Pentecostal brothers who are here. I feel we've done more than any other group in the city to quench the Spirit of God. If there is a Pentecostal brother willing to stand here at the communion table with me, I'd count it a privilege."

Moments later, the Baptist pastor was joined at the communion table by a Foursquare pastor, his Pentecostal contemporary. This man whom he had never met said with humility and grace, "Not only do I accept that apology, I want to offer an apology on behalf of the Pentecostal church for the arrogance and pride that somehow projects an attitude of superiority." Through the event, the two men became close friends and agreed to pray together every morning.[2]

Pause to consider your own reflections on confession and forgiveness.

Walking
in the Light
of God's
Son

If we confess our sins, he is faithful and just to forgive us our sins
and to cleanse us from all unrighteousness. (1 John 1:9 ESV)

Have mercy upon me, O God. According to Your lovingkindness,
according to the multitude of Your tender mercies, blot out my transgressions.
Wash me thoroughly from my iniquity, and cleanse me from my sin.
(Psalm 51:1–2)

Be still before the Lord and offer the same type of prayers that David prayed as he repented of his sin.

- *Search me, O Lord, for sins that hinder me from hearing you. Free me from all moral filth, evil, malice, deceit, hypocrisy, envy, and slander. Free me to have a cleansed heart and mind. Speak now, Lord, for I am listening.*

- *Search me, O Lord, for unresolved emotions that keep me from hearing you. Free me from any guilt or condemnation, any anger or bitterness, any fear or anxiety. Free me to live each moment in the present with you.*

- *Search me, O Lord, for childish things that distract me from hearing you. Free me from rationalizing my behavior and blaming others. Free me to practice personal responsibility before you and others.*

- *Search me, O Lord, for areas of self-focus that prevent me from hearing you. Free me from my thoughts, my ways, my ideas, and my goals. May I instead embrace your thoughts, your ways, your ideas, and your goals. Speak now, Lord, for I am listening.*

Wait before the Lord. Listen as He reveals what needs to be put away from your life.

Lord, I sense the need to put away _____
*from my life. I ask your forgiveness for holding onto this. Remove
it from my life so that I can draw closer to you.*

L-5 Living with a passionate longing for purity
and to please Him in all things

SPIRIT-
EMPOWERED
Faith

An unprecedented online partnership of 9,000 missionaries and 256 websites in 129 countries, Global Media Outreach possibly reaches 400 million people monthly with the gospel message. This far-reaching initiative is the brainchild of former Apple executive, Walt Wilson, who recalls the response of a woman half a world away. Her words after receiving the biblical account of Christ on her mobile phone were: "You are my only Christian contact. I have just prayed the prayer to receive Jesus on your website."

It's amazing what God is doing through millions of cell phones that can now transmit the gospel. Through the ministry of Global Media Outreach in 2014 alone, the good news of Jesus Christ reached 65 million Hindus and 110 million Muslims.

Clearly, digital interactive media has accelerated gospel outreach like never before, heightening the prospects of revival in our time. While the Billy Graham Evangelistic Association (BGEA) continues to preach the gospel around the world, its Internet evangelism ministry has resulted in more than eight million decisions for Christ in approximately five years. Additionally, since the BGEA launched Search for Jesus, a global multimedia Internet-infused ministry, some twenty-five million people have been exposed to the gospel. As the Internet Evangelism Director John Cass said, "Jesus' words to us were 'Go into all nations.' This technology has given us the option to go to all nations."

Dale Schlafer, and his wife, Liz, had lived in Denver for thirty-two years when he got the call. Schlafer, president of the Center for World Revival and Awakening, says, "The Lord made it very clear that we were to move to Florida because He was getting ready to do something out of the ordinary. When we arrived, we ran into people from Honduras, Guatemala, Russia, South Africa, Peru, Los Angeles, Phoenix, Chicago, Cincinnati, and New York City. All of them had been directed by God to move to the Southeast around the same time we did.

"In Florida, we found many people who had been praying for years and had visions and all kinds of things believing that this region was to become like a 'city of refuge.' Our new ministry is now bringing the church together, crossing denominational and racial divides for the work of revival, awakening, and transformation in this region. Through this work, the Lord is using us to create a template for ministry and outreach that is reproducible *in the other six continents of the world.*"

In Charlotte, North Carolina, the Transformation Church is demonstrating what it means to be a multi-ethnic, multi-generational, mission-shaped community that loves God completely (upward), loves itself correctly (inward), and loves their neighbors compassionately (outward).

"Revival is taking place with the gospel of grace," says Lead Pastor Derwin Gray. "People can experience the life of Christ in the community of Christ, and they're seeing that they can lean all of their life on Jesus. He is their peace and their righteousness."

Walking
in the Light
of God's
People

And the sheep hear his voice. (John 10:3)

Mediate quietly on Jesus as the Great Shepherd. Imagine a gentle shepherd who speaks truth in your heart and then ask Him: *Lord Jesus, what truth from your Word do you want me to experience more often? Speak, Lord; I am listening.*

Review the six Scriptures referenced below and then listen for the Spirit's leadership.

Which one of these might you need to experience more often in your life and relationships?

- Do you need to give more gentle responses, because a soft and gentle answer turns away anger (Proverbs 15:1)?

- Do you need to show more acceptance to others, just like Christ has accepted you (Romans 15:7)?

- Do you need to confess your sins to another person because a relationship needs healing (James 5:16)?

- Do you need to forgive another person, just as God forgave you (Ephesians 4:32)?

- Do you need to speak more truth in relationships or do so in a loving way (Ephesians 4:15)?

- Do you need to refrain from speaking unwholesome words and instead only share words that edify or build up (Ephesians 4:29)?

I sense it would be important for me to more often experience (which Scripture) *because* _____.

Take time to reflect on this one verse. Pray together with a partner or small group. Ask Jesus to make this verse truer in your life.

Lord Jesus, lead me beyond merely knowing the truth. Please lead me into a genuine experience of truth. I sense that your Spirit might want this verse to be particularly true of me in my relationship with _____.

Faithfully experiencing the Word makes us effective, living epistles as others take note that we have "been with Jesus!" It's this foundation of experienced truth that empowers our effective witness for Jesus.

In the course of your daily activities, listen for people who are celebrating—even the simple things. Then plan to experience Romans 12:15 with them: "Rejoice with those who rejoice."

As you listen carefully to the person's reason for celebration, be ready to rejoice.

A clerk in the grocery store might respond: "I attended our grandson's baseball tournament this weekend. It was hot but really fun!"

Your celebration response might be: "Wow! You must be so proud of him. What a terrific memory for you and your family!" Be open to further conversation as appropriate.

M-1 Imparting the gospel and one's very life in daily activities and relationships, vocation and community

SPIRIT-
EMPOWERED
Faith

A major spiritual awakening that transcends age, race, geography, denomination, income, and class is now upon us. Much like peppermint, it is spreading, and for now, it shows no signs of stopping.

As Byron Paulus, director of Life Action Ministries, says, "Much like the Wall Street collapse of 1857 that sparked the Third Great Awakening, God is getting the attention of His people in a fresh, distinct, and very important way.

"People are listening intently for answers. They're looking and searching for the truth more than they have in years. And

God's people aren't just responding on a surface-level response. They're really going deep in their heart in response to the truth and to what God could do and is doing right now."

The stories above are not previews of a coming attraction. They are real-life glimpses of real-time revival happening now, part of a Jesus-Now Awakening.

God's greatest desire, as the supreme evangelist, is for people everywhere to know Him personally in and through Jesus. Yet today, the disparity between His perfect will and His imperfect people has set the stage for God to fulfill His good and perfect will.

God has chosen to reach the rest of the world through His people, the church. Yet, for too long, the church has been corroding and weakening. You know it, and I know it. Denominational splits, unfaithful leaders, greed, sloth, single-mindedness, indifference, and pride are evidence.

No wonder our spiritual pipes have become clogged. We have been content to go on living—aware that things are not quite right—yet too lazy to do much about it.

I admit that I have participated in a church that has become corroded and impure, a church that God loves and wants to renew in what Richard Owen Roberts has so succinctly and accurately defined as "an extraordinary movement of the Holy Spirit producing extraordinary results."[3]

For God to flow through us and bring resurrection life to His church, He needs to clean out the rust. "But in a great house there are not only vessels of gold and silver, but also of wood and clay, some for honor and some for dishonor. Therefore if anyone cleanses himself from the latter, he will be a vessel for honor, sanctified and useful for the Master, prepared for every good work" (2 Timothy 2:20–21).

This purging and cleansing must occur if the Holy Spirit is to flood our nation, our churches, and our very lives. And so it begins. The first major national spiritual awakening in our country in more than 130 years is now upon us.

How have we arrived at this moment of spiritual hunger and renewal in our country?

How can we know it is real? How is this movement different from other spiritual awakenings that have swept across our country?

How can we believe there's a spiritual renewal happening if we don't see any evidence of it—especially when we're being bombarded by so much news of international terrorism, gang violence, random shootings, and moral decay?

Where is Jesus in the midst of all of this? For my family? My church? My community? Our nation? Our world?

How might Jesus want to use me in the current spiritual outpouring, reawakening, and revival?

Only Jesus can be trusted with these questions. Yet history offers a few clues for how God is now drawing His church to Himself:

- Charles Finney's "Seven Indicators" of spiritual renewal have been present in every major awakening in the United States. At least, the first four are already present in our country!
- The Bible suggests how God may usher in a national spiritual awakening in our own day. In the Old Testament, Hezekiah offers some clear parallels to our day.
- When God moves, He changes whole churches, even whole cities, in a way that impacts nations. Our nation is no exception.
- In every great spiritual awakening, as in Jesus' own day, there are spectators and participants. How close are you willing to get to Jesus to be involved in what He's already doing in our midst?

- The growing violence and darkening unrest in our nation tells us the house lights have dimmed and that the curtain is now rising on history.

Just when I am struck by the depth of our nation's sin and my own rust, God's promise becomes new again: "When I shut up heaven and there is no rain, or command the locusts to devour the land, or send pestilence among My people, if My people who are called by My name will humble themselves, and pray and seek My face, and turn from their wicked ways, then I will hear from heaven, and will forgive their sin and heal their land" (2 Chronicles 7:13–14).

Oh, for you and me to humbly pray and seek the face of God and turn from our wicked ways. For the sake of loving the One who loved us first, it can't happen soon enough.

TWO

What Is Happening to Our World?

I t happened several years ago while I was speaking at a church in Rochester, New York. The topic was church revival. For the previous four months, I had given the same presentation to church audiences of just about every denominational stripe throughout the country. I wasn't merely convinced of my message; I had become shaped by it.

"Today, there is growing evidence to suggest that we, in North America, could be on the threshold of a major spiritual awakening," I said. And with that, I launched into a carefully orchestrated outline of Scripture, complete with historical context, personal observations, and supportive media on how a new, emerging spiritual awakening in the United States was real and imminent.

After forty-five minutes, I finally took my first breath and offered to answer any questions they might have.

One woman raised her hand and then asked the question everyone was thinking, yet not dared to ask.

"Tom, I appreciate what you've said so far about the need for spiritual renewal in our country. I believe God has poured out His Spirit in extraordinary ways on different people at different points in history. I just don't buy the idea that we're in one of those times. And I'll tell you why.

"When I look around me, I see so much darkness. Families are divorcing. Young people are being ripped apart by drugs, sex, and drive-by shootings. The neighborhood, the city, the country I grew up in just doesn't exist anymore. Face it, you don't see people smile as much as they used to. Look at our world. It's filled with angry drivers, ugly graffiti, and one major world disaster after another. Starving people, terrorist-riddled lands, bankrupt, corrupt governments, and hurting friends. That's why, if you're talking about the possibility of spiritual renewal, well, it's just wishful thinking, if you ask me. How can spiritual awakening be anything more when the one thing Christians can't wait to get home for after Sunday service isn't to pray or study God's Word but to worship the Dallas Cowboys?"

Out of the corner of my eye, I could see people nodding their heads. Perhaps, the same way you're nodding "yes" right now. "Is America, on the verge of another Great Awakening, Tom? How could that possibly be when things around us are in such a mess?"

You might echo the frustration of this woman who stood up at a church seminar and said, "America's best days are behind us. From here on out, it's going to get worse." Is the darkening, troubling condition of our culture truly irreversible and irretrievable? If any leader has tried to lay claim to the word "hope," it would be Barack Obama since it was the war cry of his historic 2008 presidential election.

The president declared to an audience in Turkey that Americans "do not consider ourselves a Christian nation." If President Obama means we are indeed a people with power to reject God, then we would truly have reason to despair—ignoring, of course, the biblical promise that all the Lord does within us is according to *His* power (Ephesians 3:20). I would guess that most Christians today edge closer to Billy Graham's viewpoint. Although in 1974, Mr. Graham thought we would see another major revival in our country, ten years later he told me that he didn't see a spiritual awakening on the horizon. Instead he saw gangs, murder, and drugs—not good, but evil. Perhaps, for a moment he believed there might never be another international spiritual awakening because of such evil.

The question I asked Mr. Graham is the same one I want to ask you: Is it possible that a Jesus-Now Awakening could be different? Is it possible that evil and good will continue to grow because the Bible promises there will be a climax of both at Armageddon? After the 2011 US national elections, Billy Graham wrote an open letter to all citizens called "Fresh Vision for America," in which he stated:

Only the Gospel, God's Good News, has the power to change lives, heal hearts, and restore a nation. I want that to happen in America, and I know you want that as well. I turned ninety-four on the day after the election. Although my age and health have limited me physically in recent years, I plan to spend the next twelve months, if God permits, doing all that I am able to do in helping to carry out a fresh vision God has given us—a vision to bring the Gospel of Jesus Christ to every possible place in America by the time of my ninety-fifth birthday. It's called *My Hope*, and I pray that you will partner.

In the days of the prophet Jeremiah, God commanded His people to "seek the peace and prosperity" of the land where He had placed them and to "pray to the LORD for it" (Jeremiah 29:7 NIV). I ask you to join me in committing the next fifty-two weeks to faithful, even fervent, prayer for this land in which we live. You can start by making a list of people you know personally who need Jesus Christ and then begin praying regularly for them, individually by name.

Pray also for your neighborhood and your city, asking God to bring men, women, teens, and children—people from your own community—to Himself during the next twelve months. And pray along with me for the nation, asking God for mercy on America and for a great spiritual awakening.[1]

Walking in the Light of God's People

So don't be surprised when I say,
"You must be born again." (John 3:7 NLT)

This discourse between Jesus and Nicodemus has personal relevance to each of us. It's this experience of being born again that makes us part of His family, a shared community of Jesus-followers.

Just like Nicodemus, we have been challenged to embrace Jesus as more than a teacher and to receive Him as Lord. We, like Nicodemus, have been provided the opportunity to add His supernatural life to our natural life. It's this miracle of being "Spirit-born" that unites us by the Holy Spirit both to Jesus and to one another. It's the connection of the born-again that creates true fellowship, a community of Spirit-empowered followers who embrace the imperative to "let us run with endurance the race set before us, looking unto Jesus, the author and finisher of *our* faith" (Hebrews 12:1–2). The pursuit of revival and a Jesus-Now Awakening is for *us*, not a solo race, but for a community of Jesus-followers who co-labor with Him for His purposes and His glory.

Pause together with a partner or small group.

Share your personal stories of being "born again" into the family of God.

Celebrate together that His Spirit brings new birth to all kinds of people. Celebrate that you can each be a part of all the great things God is up to!

P-7 Expecting and demonstrating the supernatural as His spiritual gifts are made manifest and His grace is at work by His Spirit

The early signs of a Jesus-Now Awakening in our country are mere pinpoints of light in a darkening landscape; these are pinpoints of light that can be seen only when everything else is black—pinpoints of light whose gleaming presence is a brilliant reminder that darkness has never been able to overcome light. This conviction was illustrated for me in a frightening experience I had as a teenager.

When I was eighteen, my friend Clay Crockett and I decided to explore a cave near the Tennessee River. We entered the tunnel with the bravado of Indiana Jones. After walking twenty minutes or so, all signs of natural light had vanished behind us. This wasn't a problem until our one flashlight died. Clay claimed he knew the path back out. I wanted to believe him. Oh, how I wanted to believe him! I could feel the sweat bead up on the back of my neck as I held up my hand in front of my face ... but saw nothing. We knew there was a large, deep well in the cave, somewhere.

There was only blackness and thick, dank air.

The only way out was to crawl. There I was, walking on my hands and knees, checking the ground inch-by-inch. Clay was behind, walking stooped, holding on to my belt, and leaning backwards. Ten minutes. Twenty minutes. With sharp edges of rock digging into my kneecaps, I lost track of time. Since we simply backed up and retraced our route, I had to believe we were going in the right direction. Belief was all we had; our eyes were wide open, yet our world was pitch black.

I don't recall which of us saw it first—a speck of something white. It was light, smaller than a dust particle, and it came and went just like that. Yet this tiny pinprick of light was huge, because it meant we were headed in the right direction! There *was* a way out of the cave, and we were on that one and only path.

This is how I believe the coming spiritual awakening will occur, by defining the lines of darkness and light. The contrasts will be so sharp, the evidence of the Lord so clear, that no world leader, no movement, no organization or coalition will be able to take credit for such an obvious spiritual transformation. Like people lost in a cave surrounded by darkness, we will know that there can only be one explanation: God Himself.

Today, compared to twenty years ago, we are seeing a return to prayer, confession, and the emergence of a new spiritual hunger that's more than a mere pinprick. It is God's light shining in the hearts of His people, the church, much like creation when "the earth was without form, and void; and darkness was on the face of the deep" (Genesis 1:2).

God is at work again, not dispelling darkness completely, but rather piercing it to dispel its presence. Pockets of light are now appearing throughout our society in this Jesus-Now Awakening.

How will we be able to see this? How will we be able to realize that God is working, not only in the midst of darkness to revive Christians with renewed life, but also through such a revival to bring new life to those who are yet to believe? We know it because this is the promise of Psalm 67:2: "That Your way may be known on earth, Your salvation among all nations."

God's constant re-creative nature to rekindle His people, and through them, to light that same fire in others who have known only darkness, is undeniable and ready to emerge again in our time. The question is, "Will we choose to be part of it?" More basic than this is, "Will we be able to recognize such a renewal as it unfolds before us?" And finally, "Will we—each of us—join Jesus and get involved in what He's already doing?"

The present revival I'm talking about is so different and so radically life-transforming—unlike the world we live in today— that the only way to see this spiritual movement is with a new set of eyes, different from the ones you and I were given at birth. It's only with spiritual eyes able to spot and follow a pinprick of light that you and I will be able to see beyond this present darkness. Only when we know this truth will we see that this current speck of God's light is much bigger, much brighter, than our world's current darkness.

David Bryant is a former pastor, minister-at-large for Intervarsity Christian Fellowship and founder of Concerts of Prayer International. Today, he is lead facilitator for Proclaim HOPE!, which is dedicated exclusively to "fostering and serving a nationwide Christ-awakening movement, the God-given hope for which multitudes currently are praying around the world."[2]

In the Holy Scriptures, hope is a noun; hope is a Person. This hope, as revival, is a hope that's so compelling, so wonderful you can't live without it, but yet so wonderful you know you can't produce it. In light of this hope, we're not purpose-driven. We're person-driven—the person of Jesus Christ. We need a large enough vision of Jesus, His love and salvation, that ignites fresh hope and passion toward Him and then begins to "reconvert" God's people back to God's Son for all that He is. This is what comes out of true spiritual awakening, true revival—sustained transformation both inside the church and through the church.[3]

Walking in the Light of God's Son

Have I been with you so long, and yet you have not known Me...? (John 14:9)

A life of revival requires fresh, frequent encounters with Jesus to empower and motivate our partnership with Jesus as an "awakening catalyst." Spend the next few moments reflecting on this truth. Could it be that one of the reasons there's not more hope, not more experience of revival in our nation, is that the people of Jesus don't really know Him? If we commit to knowing Jesus deeply, personally, and in fresh, new ways, we'll be compelled to share our hope in Him.

Consider what it must do to the heart of Jesus for His people not to truly know Him. What does it do to your heart to imagine Jesus speaking these same words to you?

Dear one, I've been with you all this time and you still don't know who I am. You don't really know me. I long for you to know me, so that together we can transform a world.

Tell Jesus about the impact His words have on your heart.

Jesus, as I sense your sadness that your followers have often missed knowing you, my heart feels. ... As I seek to live a life of revival and blessing, prompt me often, Holy Spirit, to consistently pursue a deeper knowing of Jesus.

L-3 Experiencing God as He really is through deepened intimacy with Him

SPIRIT-EMPOWERED Faith

Every Christian leader with whom I've talked, including David Bryant, has identified and reaffirmed that something new and powerful from God is going on in America. Each of them also can point to his own distinctive moment of spiritual awakening.

My understanding of revival has been shaped by being personally humbled through my own broken pride. It happened on a painful afternoon in Asheville, North Carolina, in 1988. Up to that time, my life had been filled with accomplishment and praise. The day my personal pride crumbled was the day I started to see God's extraordinary character, in some ways for the first time.

I grew up in the farmland of northern Mississippi, in a loving Christian family. My dad was a soldier then a carpenter. Eventually, he owned half a dozen businesses, including a gas station. When I was eight years old—the same year I became a Christian—he had the best help a father could hope for, an eager son who was willing to do almost anything he asked. If a customer rolled in with a dirty windshield, I'd wash it. If my uncles—who picked cotton all day in the hot sun—were hungry and thirsty, I took them lunch and a gallon jug of ice water wrapped in old newspaper. I was obedient. I never remember lying. I never smoked nor drank (except for a sip of warm beer when I was ten, which was the last time I touched the bottle!).

When I was twelve our family moved to the city, and I became a nobody. My pants were too small and tight; my shirt was uncool. The best conversations I had were with myself. Books became my best friends, and my nickname became "Encyclopedia." With the help of a college scholarship, I was going to medical school. Two years into my studies, I couldn't ignore a question that had been hounding me. Finally, one night, it caught up to me: "What's more important, saving a life so that a person can live another seventy or eighty years on earth or helping save a soul for eternity?" By the stairway of a friend's apartment, I fell to my knees and began to weep. I had heard my calling. My heart was tied to helping people know God's love.

In 1974, I began working with Billy Graham. I helped direct evangelistic crusades in the United States and Europe and oversaw efforts in counseling and follow-up. Never in my life had I faced such fulfilling and demanding work. Thankfully, there was a spiritual mentor, Charlie Riggs, who guided me through the rapids and torrents that inevitably came. With the staff I eventually guided and served, I sought to dispense the credit to others rather than claim it for myself. My management philosophy was not "me" but "we." In fact, for a long period of time, I wouldn't write a letter with "I" in it.

Yet I had my flaws. I knew I had a large ego. Awareness finally came when I was perched at the highest level of responsibility I had ever attained. I was to be director of a new center to train and send evangelists throughout the world. All of my study, training, and ministry had prepared me for this moment. Then, as soon as my vision started to come together, the whole thing began to unravel. Mixed messages from various people, responsibilities not clarified, expectations not met, all conspired to undo the situation.

Everything I had prepared for, worked for, lived for in ministry was not to be. Not in this "opportunity."

That's when a gray sense of despair began to press in. Against my nature, I took pills to help me sleep, but they did no good. I was Mr. Obedient, and against my character, I wanted out—out of the religious politics that had always engulfed others, out of the compromising character of others. On a few terribly lonely nights, I thought I wanted out of life, not because I wanted to commit suicide, but because I wanted to be with Christ, someone who was perfect, pure, and loved me unconditionally.

On that painful afternoon in 1988, three thousand miles from my wife and family, I sat by myself in a small hotel room. The pressure to make good on my ministry commitment, knowing I wasn't wanted or valued, refused to go away. Stress quickly became depression. It came not from the outside, but from within, attaching itself to my soul like a bloated leech—a terrible, dark feeling without bottom or end.

I remember the exact moment my panic reached its peak. I rushed over to the only window in the room thinking, *What am I going to do?* I looked outside. I had to see something that was alive, something that could break through my darkness. I gazed through the window but there was no one in sight—just vegetation, a hillside with bushes, and a tree. Praise God for that single tree! As I saw the wind rustle through its upper leaves, I saw *life*.

I must have stared at it for a long time, for at that moment, surrounded by the blackness within me, this tree was the only living thing I knew. Without warning, the picture changed. A bird flew toward the tree and lightly perched on one of its top branches. Immediately, something happened inside me.

For the first time in days, perhaps weeks, I felt life surging within me. Life unexpectedly trickled back into my black world. I thanked God for this tiny bird because through it I was seeing life overcome death in me. I knew I couldn't stop looking until all the mental blackness went away. After three or four minutes of silence, of praying and trusting God, the blackness faded. Looking back, it's as if I had yielded myself to the Lord in a fresh way, allowing Him to bring a renewed sense of a Jesus-Now Awakening into my life.

A month and a half later, I resigned my position. I had accomplished what I had been asked to do. Outwardly, it was a cordial departure; inside, I felt terribly wounded. If you've ever been moved aside, let go, passed over, or simply ignored—and you know you've done all the right things that were humanly possible at the time—then you know the kind of circumstance I'm describing. In your mind, it can all make sense, but nothing, it seems, can take away the hurt.

For years, I had prayed, "God, make me more like Christ." For years, I had been so confident. I was the clay on the potter's wheel, so sure that I was going to be molded into positions of greater and greater responsibility. After all, I knew, with Him, I couldn't fail. And yet, I had. Why? Why would this God I had served and loved for so many years want to break me?

"O house of Israel, can I not do with you as this potter?' says the LORD. "Look, as the clay *is* in the potter's hand, so *are* you in My hand, O house of Israel!" (Jeremiah 18:6).

I knew the Scripture. Since I knew clay didn't control the potter's wheel, I could only do one thing: pray to the Master Potter that He might mold me to be more like Christ. For years, He had been working to shape my character, so flawed by prideful imperfections I couldn't see. Why would God allow me to be broken at the height of my ministry career? Why would He push down the clay of my life and remold me?

The only answer I can give is that I had prayed to be a vessel, *His* vessel. "Therefore if anyone cleanses himself from the latter, he will be a vessel for honor, sanctified and useful for the Master, prepared for every good work" (2 Timothy 2:21). For years—through seminary, in early churches I pastored, and through global evangelistic efforts—I had been lifted up by others, only to find that the vessel did not control the potter. While being grateful to God, I was still proud of the vessel. I remained unconscious of a deeper truth going on at the time. All I saw were immediate benefits and the next logical rung on the ladder of my resume. I couldn't see the hairline cracks in my own character. Had I stepped into the fire of the new position I wanted so badly, the vessel that God had spent years shaping would have been blown apart.

Consequently, in His own way, God did a very loving thing. He allowed me to go through a severe breaking and has done so several times. He cut short my dream that His will could be fulfilled. He could have made the correction silently and painlessly so I wouldn't have felt a thing. (That would have been my choice!) However (and here's His great patience and love at work), He allowed the process to be turbulent enough that I was forced to sit up and take notice. He allowed me to feel my self-satisfied ego and other personality flaws being crushed.

Alone with myself, I cried to Jesus.

Alone with the sight of a simple tree, I began to live.

Alone with God, I saw the wisdom of the Master Potter. He didn't take me off the wheel and give up on me!

Because of that dark day in Asheville, I once more rejoiced in ministry. I got in touch with my most obvious flaws and I confessed them before God, not knowing that my own personal revival had begun. I had joined Jesus passionately and purposefully in His Jesus-Now Awakening.

Walking
in the Light
of God's
Word

He must become greater and greater,
and I must become less and less. (John 3:30 NLT)

This passage of Scripture reveals a critical imperative to living a life of personal revival. It will require a two-dimensional imperative: He must increase, and I must decrease!

The imperative is not just for John the Baptist but for each Spirit-empowered follower. Practically though, what does it look like for Jesus to gain prominence? Think about your daily living, your thoughts and activities, your attitudes and priorities. Scripture reminds us that:

- His thoughts are higher than our thoughts (Isaiah 55:8).
- His activity is characterized by the fruit of the Spirit and never the deeds of the flesh (Galatians 5:19–23).

- His attitude is characterized by humility and thinking more highly of others (Philippians 2:3).
- His priorities focus on loving His Father, loving people, and imparting the gospel that others might embrace Him and these priorities (Matthew 22:37–40, 28:19–20).

As Jesus continues to increase, and we continue to decrease, every part of our lives will be impacted.

Pause and reflect on these sentences. Celebrate any evidence of how Jesus is increasing:

- *I recently was having more of His thoughts as I …*
- *Recently, in my daily activity, I sensed the fruit of His Spirit when …*
- *His attitude of humility and thinking of others was evident recently as I …*
- *His priority of loving God and other people was expressed recently when …*
- His priority of sharing my life and the gospel was recently demonstrated as I …

Celebrate one or more of these evidences of His increase and then pray for one another. Pray that these changes will continue and that each of you will decrease because a Jesus-Now Awakening is characterized by evidences of His thinking and activity, His attitude and priorities.

W-6 Encountering Jesus in the Word for deepened transformation in Christ-likeness

Whether you believe a major spiritual awakening is present, unfolding, or still somewhere in the distance, it's difficult to deny that God is drawing His people to Himself and that His people are poised to reach others with Christ. There's hope for those in spiritual darkness.

If the current flicker, perhaps glow, of God's light leads to a widespread spiritual awakening in this country, will we look back and realize God began His work through unlikely individuals who were simply broken and humbled? Isn't it interesting that personal humility has always been a prerequisite of major Christian leaders and the movements their faith has inspired?

- Dietrich Bonhoeffer, scribbling a diary of costly discipleship in a dim German jail, knew that his execution was only days away.
- Martin Luther King Jr. resisted a life of demeaning slur and the fire hoses of angry whites with non-violent love.
- Mother Teresa, living a quiet discipline of poverty in a Hungarian convent, prepared herself for the day she would pick up the first of an estimated twenty-six thousand beggars from the gutters of Calcutta.

Each leader was humiliated, emptied of self, and brought to the admission that "I *have* nothing because before you, I *am* nothing; therefore, anything I own, anything I do, anything I hope to become can come only from you alone."

Isn't it interesting that in these three classic examples, we see God using broken people who live and work in the midst of needy and (in some cases) desperate surroundings? If a major spiritual awakening does take place in our country, will it be because God makes His will known, not in the absence of evil's influence, but in the midst of an ever-darkening world?

- Before 1988, few Christians in Portland held out much hope that area pastors could ever reconcile their long and bitter denominational disputes. How humorous (and how like God!) that a model for pastoral reconciliation and renewal would spring up in Oregon, a state that's home to the nation's highest proportion of people without a God-based value system!

- In 1995, pastors and congregations from 100 churches throughout New York City began a 24/7 prayer vigil. During the next five years, the murder rate in the city dropped by 70 percent. Mac Pier, president of the New York City Leadership Center, who has been at the center of this devoted effort, believes there is a parallel relationship between the ongoing prayer movement and church planting. From 2008–2010, ten denominations, working together, have helped incubate 100 new churches in New York City. "As pastors began to pray together, they began to trust each other. This is probably the greatest outcome of the prayer movement."[4]

- A church in Memphis, where spiritual awakening has stirred, grew out of an inner-city mission to the down-and-out. Sixty-five percent of the church's original members came out of alcohol- and drug-related backgrounds. After a church leader confessed to adultery at a Saturday breakfast meeting, a number of elders came forward and did the same. One man's personal revival speaks into other broken lives. Within the dark cave of sin, a stark confession shines the light of God's forgiveness into a new repentant heart.

- In the summer of 2014, in Ferguson, Missouri, Michael Brown, an eighteen-year-old, black man, was fatally shot by Darren Wilson, a twenty-eight-year-old white Ferguson police officer. Brown's death, surrounded by conflicting evidence and disputed circumstances, ignited both violent and peaceful protests in Ferguson, around St. Louis, and throughout the country. Later, Rev. Renita Marie Lamkin, pastor of St. John's African

Methodist Episcopal Church in St. Charles, Missouri, concluded her "Collective Prayer for Ferguson" this way:

> We shed these tears not in despair but with hope. We scream not just in anger but in fear, realizing that because we live in a world where many have time to hate, there will be a next time. Hear our cries, "We are sick and tired of being sick and tired." Embrace us in arms of peace. "No guilt in life, no fear in death. This is the power of Christ in me. From life's first cry to final breath, Jesus commands my destiny."

As the culture moves away from its Judeo-Christian roots, more and more people appear to recognize the devastation of sin and are turning to the good news of the gospel. They cry out to be saved from themselves and be secure in Christ.

While we do not see swells of genuine revival sweeping across our country, I do see something nearly as significant: pockets of broken, humble people in less-than-perfect conditions who, both individually and corporately, are beginning to experience the fullness of God in ways most believers of our nation have never approached. Their willingness to pray, to confess their sins to each other and to the Lord, and to remain in awe of God alone as the author of this new movement, is exactly what the Lord had in mind when He made His famous promise to Solomon: "If My people who are called by My name will humble themselves, and pray and seek My face, and turn from their wicked ways, then I will hear from heaven, and will forgive their sin and heal their land. Now *My eyes will be open and My ears attentive to prayer made in this place* (2 Chronicles 7:14–15).

In a word, this is God's desire both for Solomon's era and for ours. He longs for us to experience a true, personal, spiritual awakening. I don't mean a pre-planned, sawdust-trail event, but an awakening in the fullest meaning of the word "revival," which in the Old Testament meant "to wake up and live."

Who wouldn't want this today? Who wouldn't want to see beyond the evil in our nation, to know revival as Robert Coleman has described it so infectiously: "breathing in the breath of God"?

You have already met a few people, who now are experiencing this new life, and you will meet others. As you see Jesus draw each man and woman to Himself, I believe you will see how prayer, public confession, and an ever-humbling awe of God have preceded every major revival in America.

When you read about the crime, moral unraveling, and spiritual deadness that led up to these spiritual awakenings, you will think history is repeating itself in our time. And you would be right. Maybe such darkness is merely the backdrop for glimmers of light, emerging from the life and love of true Christ-followers in this Jesus-Now Awakening.

THREE

A Truth
We Almost Forgot

Look around your neighborhood. On the surface, nothing seems to have changed much in the past several years. The streets look the same, so do the houses. Sure, there's more congestion, but that's what you would expect with growth.

Yet appearances can be deceptive. Remember when you used to take a nice evening walk? In some locales, those days are gone. They ended when the crime you had been reading about for years began to invade *your* neighborhood. Now, the news of random break-ins in our nation has given way to new, growing threats— Ebola, global economic instability, corruption, injustice, and the next terrorist attack.

In such a climate, you might think that churches would be growing, and some are. Yet many longstanding denominations are losing members. Giving is down. Operational budgets and mission programs are hurting. The same people who smile and shake the pastor's hand at the door see society unraveling before their eyes with no turnaround in sight. All the things that could ignite hope for positive change—the Bible, prayer, Sunday worship—are labeled irrelevant and lifeless by outsiders. They not only question Christianity but hold the church and often pastors in contempt. On the other end of the national landscape, Christians look at a morally adrift, self-centered culture and ask, "How far can all this go?"

IT'S HAPPENED BEFORE

You might be surprised to learn that Americans were asking just such a question in 1794! If you think our current moral decay, increasing violence, and crumbling ethics are signs of an inevitable, darker, downward spiral, think again. Consider the uneasy twilight of the late eighteenth century. Illegitimate births were rampant. Alcohol, the drug of the day, was destroying families and wrecking futures. Thomas Paine was proclaiming that Christianity was dead—and certainly, the body of faith appeared to be in a coma.

Yet even as church rolls were shrinking and greed, sensuality, and family breakdown were becoming more widespread, America was about to experience a great spiritual revival.

It would start small, in a handful of broken-down corners of society with a few people praying. In one year, it would spread like a wildfire through churches, seminaries, and families, changing the spiritual landscape of entire cities and towns. People would spend days and nights in prayer and worship. Christians, who believed God had given up on their nation, saw thousands of people, who admitted they were dead inside and who found new life through forgiveness, wrapped in a power they had never seen. This phenomenon would unfold for the next forty-five years. Although it was the first time America had experienced revival, it would not be the last.

How do we make sense of the growing evidence that our country and our continent could be ripe for a major spiritual awakening? The late evangelist Bob Cryder suggested, "If revival happens in the sanctuary (and we're beginning to see isolated cases), then we're standing in the foyer." Today, an increasing number of Christians, including myself, believe we're *that* close.

Four times in history, God's Spirit of revival has touched our nation and transformed its people:

- The Great Awakening (1730–1743)
- The Second Great Awakening (1800–1830)
- The Third Great Awakening (1857–1859)
- The Fourth Great Awakening (1960–1970)

The elements that led to each movement bear a strange resemblance to events that have taken place in the dawn of a new millennium.

Now, as then, Christian leaders are being brought to their knees through humble, public confession. Around the United States, in a growing number of pockets, prayer is exploding. People of all economic, racial, and denominational hues are turning back to God. Clearly, the spiritual hunger of our day offers conspicuous clues to historic parallels that cannot be denied. It is time we looked at:

- The unique, yet strangely similar, qualities of America's major revivals that parallel what's currently happening in individual lives, churches, prayer groups, and homes.
- The amazing consistency in the blessings that revival produced in Old Testament times—the same blessings our nation so desperately needs today.
- The seven indicators that reveal, not so much how close or far away we may be from experiencing revival, but how God is now calling people to Himself.

Let's look more closely at each of these points. Let's resist the temptation to forecast when or if revival will happen in our country. Instead, let's spend a moment with history. If our spiritual eyes are open, we may begin to see how Jesus Now is impacting our land. And as we begin to look, let's pray a prayer, patterned after some wise men from the tribe of Issachar: "Oh, God, make us men and women who understand the times so that we may know what we ought to do" (1 Chronicles 12:32).

Walking in the Light of God's Son

Then Jesus spoke to them again, saying,
"I am the light of the world. He who follows Me shall not walk
in darkness, but have the light of life." (John 8:12)

In John 8:12–30, Jesus asserts that He is the light of the world and then lets the disciples know that He's not even from this world! In His encounter with religious leaders, Jesus spoke to His identity, background, and purpose. Jesus also offers hope to those of us who follow Him. Our hope for revival and awakening is found in the God-man, Jesus.

Jesus boldly proclaimed that He is "the light of the world," so as we encounter Him and experience His love, we experience one source of God's transforming light (Psalm 36:9, John 12:35).

God, the Father, is longing for us to pursue Jesus, because He delights in revealing more of Himself to us. Whether through worship, prayer, meditation and study, or through the mundane happenings of everyday life, Jesus wants to be known by you!

In what ways has the Lord revealed Himself to you? Has Jesus revealed His wisdom, His nature, His loving concern, and His character to you? In what ways has He made Himself known?

I have recently encountered God's Son, Jesus, by _____

_____

_____

_____.

(For example: I have recently encountered God's Son, Jesus, by picturing Him praying for me, especially during a time when I was feeling very lonely.)

Pause and pray with a partner or small group to rejoice in your identity as a friend of Jesus. Give Him thanks that your hope is in Him.

L-1 Practicing thanksgiving in all things

THE FIRST GREAT AWAKENING

You don't have to listen too hard to make out the cries of harried Americans today. Pressed by too many demands, too little time, mushrooming pressures, and shrinking paychecks, people are quick to confess, "I'm just trying to survive." That's exactly what Americans were saying in the days that led to our nation's first Great Awakening. Forced with building a society from scratch, the early settlers defined the word "pressure." Pressure didn't come from daily freeway commutes or seventy-hour workweeks but from fighting medical emergencies without the ability to dial 911 and winters without cozy, insulated homes. Crops failed, diseases spread, and early deaths were common.

Where was the church in all of this? In 1606, the First Charter of Virginia articulated the deeply held Christian principles of our nation's founders:

We, greatly commending, and graciously accepting of, their Desires for the Furtherance of so noble a Work, which may, by the Providence of Almighty God, hereafter tend to the Glory of His Divine Majesty, in propagating of Christian Religion to such People, as yet live in Darkness and miserable Ignorance of the true Knowledge and Worship of God, and may in time bring the Infidels and Savages, living in those Parts, to human Civility, and to a settled and quiet Government.[1]

By the century's end, however, something had been lost. Thanks to the Halfway Covenant, a person could belong to a church without believing in Jesus Christ for salvation. The Halfway Covenant allowed unbelieving children of believing parents to receive baptism; they simply weren't allowed to receive the Lord's Supper or vote on church matters. Thus was faith reduced to a formality. People lived with growing irreverence, succumbed to rampant dishonesty, and grew reluctant to acknowledge the word "sin."

Jonathan Edwards, perhaps the greatest theologian our country has ever produced, "lamented the deterioration of society. He wrote that even 'children were given to night waking and tavern haunting.'"[2]

Into such a dismal cultural climate, a spiritual outbreak occurred which no one could have predicted—the Great Awakening. On one Sunday, Theodore J. Frelinghuysen, a twenty-nine-year-old pietist, preached what few wanted to admit: Human beings were depraved and needed a personal encounter with God and a change of heart. But it was Edwards' preaching that reverberated in the hearts and minds of his hearers. When he asked his congregation, "How many kinds of wickedness are there?" he didn't wait for a response. He simply described what he saw all around him—irreverence in God's house, disregard of the Sabbath, neglect of family prayer, disobedience to parents, quarreling, greediness, sensuality, and hatred of one's neighbor.[3]

Edwards had the holy nerve to weave his accurate assessment

into a gripping word picture that showed people they were as helpless to do anything about their own sinful condition as insects dangling over an open flame: "You hang by a slender thread, with the flames of divine wrath flashing about it, and ready every moment to singe and burn it asunder; and you have nothing to lay hold of to save yourself, nothing to keep off the flames of wrath, nothing of your own, nothing that you have ever done, nothing that you can do to induce God to spare you one moment."[4]

The effect of Edwards' sermon set New England ablaze. Men and women wept tears of deep remorse. They knew they needed to be forgiven. They came to God on their knees, and out of their deep sorrow and repentance, they received an unexpected feeling of cleansing and joy. What was dead came to life.

Spiritual night was nailed beneath the floor of spiritual dawn. The new fervor spread to a hundred communities. Nearly 300 people—25 percent of 1,100 individuals in his town alone—were then converted. The Great Awakening witnessed an immediate, overt transformation in men and women throughout New England. People felt deep conviction when they realized they had turned their backs on God. Guilt led to confession, confession led to forgiveness, and forgiveness led to new devotion to a Lord and Savior thousands had never known.

By 1735, the Great Awakening began to cool. It might have ended altogether had it not been for George Whitefield. If Edwards was the spark of revival, Whitefield became the flame that forced the movement to spread. In thirty-two years in the mid-1700s, this Englishman made seven trips to America to preach. His style was dramatic and pointed. "I love those who thunder out the word," he said. "The Christian world is in a dead sleep. Nothing but a loud voice can awaken them out of it."[5]

By 1760, few were still asleep. During the Great Awakening,

an estimated 25,000 to 50,000 people became believers. One hundred and fifty new Congregational churches were founded. Separatists, Baptists, and Presbyterian churches multiplied—over 10 percent of New England's total population of no more than 340,000. That equates to approximately 30 million citizens today.[6]

By the time the flame of the Great Awakening began to die out for good in 1760, thousands of people who once had turned their back on God had changed their way of living. From New England to the colony of Jamestown, where the people's indifference to the Bible had been strong, conversions to Christ were so remarkable it was agreed that only God could have brought about such a sweeping transformation. To some, the revival must have seemed total and final. Never again, would they face such desperate spiritual poverty. They believed, never again, could things get so bad. In a way, they were right. Forty years later, the situation would be even worse.

THE SECOND GREAT AWAKENING

By 1800, the American church was in trouble again. The Revolutionary War had inflicted serious damage on believing communities. Scores of congregations that had sided with the British had lost their prestige. Others were scattered, and many of those still intact had been left without pastors. In a war fought, in part, to protect religious freedom, church buildings had been dismantled or used as barracks or stables.

The real casualties were the people. Worship waned and immorality flourished. As the survivalist mentality moved westward into Appalachia, spiritual basics of Bible reading and prayer were left behind. Colleges such as Yale, Princeton, and William and Mary—centers of learning that had been founded on Christian belief—now disowned their charters.

Orthodox faith was swept aside by rationalism. In the mind of Thomas Jefferson and other influential thinkers, reason left little room for a creator intimately involved with people. To the deist, God had wound up the universe and put the clock in our hands. If an individual or society grew, it wasn't because God guided, intervened, or empowered; it was because people exercised their rational, human minds. Rationalism's rise made faith a white elephant. The results were devastating. Episcopalian Devereaux Jarret wrote, "The state of religion is gloomy and distressing; the church of Christ seems to have sunk very low."[7] Kenneth Scott Latourette, the great church historian, proclaimed, "It seemed as if Christianity were about to be ushered out of the affairs of men."[8] United States Chief Justice John Marshall wrote this obituary: "The church is too far gone ever to be redeemed."[9]

Yet the bleak moral and spiritual outlook became a blessing in disguise. Christians felt so low there was nowhere to look but up. Baptist minister Isaac Backus said, "There's only one power on earth that commands the power of heaven—prayer."[10] In 1794, he mailed letters pleading with pastors to set aside the first Monday of each month to pray. The response was overwhelming. Within a short time, Baptists, Presbyterians, Congregationalists, Reformed, and Moravians were joined in a national movement of prayer. Throughout the frontiers of Ohio, Kentucky, and Tennessee, prayer groups sprang up.

Rationally speaking, nothing should have come from it, especially in places like Logan County, Kentucky. This sordid haven for criminals, robbers, and vigilantes lived up to its name: Rogue's Harbor. While constantly praying for spiritual awakening to shake the town, a Presbyterian minister named James McGready, conducted a community-wide communion service in 1800. Later that year, he held another Lord's Supper during a weekend, and eleven thousand people flocked to the tiny Gasper

River Presbyterian Church. Some came from as far as one hundred miles away. McGready wrote down what transpired when William McGee, a Presbyterian pastor, delivered a sermon based on Peter who set out to walk on water toward Jesus:

> The power of God seemed to shake the whole assembly. Towards the close of the sermon, the cries of the distressed arose almost as loud as his voice. After the congregation was dismissed the solemnity increased, till the greater part of the multitude seemed engaged in the most solemn manner. No person seemed to wish to go home—hunger and sleep seemed to affect nobody—eternal things were the vast concern. Here awakening and converting work was to be found in every part of the multitude; and even some things strangely and wonderfully new to me. [11]

It was only a prelude to what took place one year later in Cane Ridge, Kentucky, where ten- to twenty-five thousand men, women, and children gathered to worship and pray. The gathering was so large, yet so united, that four to five preachers, standing on stumps of recently hewn trees, spoke at the same time. Denominational differences melted into a display of emotion that had never before been seen. One person present said that eight hundred persons "were struck down," lying incoherent on the ground for minutes, even hours.[12] James Finley, who later became a circuit-riding preacher, described the sound "like the roar of Niagara. ... At one time I saw at least five hundred swept down in a moment as if a battery of a thousand guns had been opened upon them, and then immediately followed shrieks and shouts that rent the very heavens."[13] Such was the power of spiritual conviction.

When George Baxter, president of Washington College in

Virginia, rode through the same region of Kentucky some months later, he called it:

> The most moral place I have ever seen. ... A religious awe seemed to pervade the country. ... Upon the whole, I think the revival in Kentucky the most extraordinary that has ever visited the church of Christ. ... Infidelity was triumphant, and religion was on the point of expiring. Something extraordinary seemed necessary to arrest the attention of a giddy people who were ready to conclude that Christianity was a fable. ... This revival has done it! It has confounded infidelity, awed vice into sitting and brought numbers beyond calculation under serious impression.[14]

The facts bore this out. On the sparsely populated frontiers of our country, the number of Methodist Wesleyan believers increased almost fivefold from twenty-seven hundred to twelve thousand. From 1799 to 1803, an estimated ten thousand people joined the Baptist church. The revival gave birth to a new interest in missions and organizations such as the American Bible Society and the American Sunday School Union.

By its very name, the Second Great Awakening proved that revival could happen again. If evangelism was an ongoing command, revival was a periodic movement meant to bring a people back into a right relationship with God. Some at the time concluded that revival—the presence and power of Christ that gives a person meaning, direction, purpose, and hungering for more of God— was (and is) a return to normal Christianity. (I also believe this.) Though this context and expression were vastly different from the spiritual revolution of Edwards' and Whitefield's day, the revival of 1800 startled thousands of families, churches, and Christian leaders out of their spiritual slumber. They came to the same conclusion that had once sustained their spiritual ancestors—in the midst of a nation's darkness, those who know they're lost will be able to see the pinhole of light that cuts through darkness to a loving God.

If the First Great Awakening responded to a lack of truth, the Second Great Awakening corrected the untruth of skeptical rationalism. Cane Ridge showed that God could change a community overnight. The real story was not emotionalism *per se*. The real story was that the dramatic outpouring of remorse, confession, and faith matched the depth of a previously hardened people's longing for a God they had abandoned. The Second Great Awakening showed that regardless of how far a nation had drifted from God, God could breathe new life into repentant people and revive their nation. America's new spirit of Christian devotion was so strong, some thought it would never end. But then, these people were not living in the city where a third Great Awakening was about to take place.

THE THIRD GREAT AWAKENING

This is how Baptist preacher and author Dr. J. Edwin Orr described America in the 1850s:

- Gambling, gain, and greed are widespread, with a rapid increase in violent crime.
- The occult dominates in a nation hungry for the supernatural. Spiritism has gained a popular foothold over many minds.
- A playboy philosophy of "free love" is advocated and accepted by many.
- Commercial and political corruption is epidemic. Bribes, graft, and illegal business practices are rife in the nation.

- Atheism, agnosticism, apathy, and indifference to God, to the church and its message are omnipresent. The decline is fourfold: social, moral, political, and spiritual.[15]

Such was the culture that swirled outside the North Dutch Reformed Church building in New York City in the fall of 1857. The church had hired Jeremiah Lanphier to influence the surrounding area for the gospel. Fifteen years earlier, Lanphier had come to Christ at a tabernacle constructed by Charles Finney.[16] Lanphier, a forty-year-old businessman, invited people to join him for a noontime prayer meeting on Thursday, September 23. He canvassed the downtown industrial corridor for weeks, inviting people to attend.

The big day came, and by 12:30 p.m. no one had arrived. By 1:00 p.m. six people were present. The turnout encouraged Lanphier to hold a second meeting. The next Wednesday, twenty people came to pray. The third week, there were forty.

Then, on October 14, the worst financial crisis in the nation's history hit. Banks closed their doors. People lost their jobs. Families went hungry. At Lanphier's Fulton Street meeting, more than three thousand people crowded in to pray. Six months later, ten thousand businessmen in New York City were gathering in groups for daily prayer.

During the next two years, one million people throughout the United States—one-thirtieth of the entire population—committed themselves to Jesus Christ. The Fulton Street Revival spread throughout the country. Out of the "Great Prayer Revival of 1857–59," or Third Great Awakening, thousands of people—physicians, lawyers, accountants, and scores of men, women, and families—came to new life in Jesus.

Only one explanation has ever been given for such phenomenal spiritual impact—prayer. Prayer was what a layman, named

Jeremiah Lanphier, knew would reach God. Prayer was what drew the first trickle of people to his third-floor office. Prayer was what caused hundreds and thousands of people, many who had never seen the inside of a church, to fall to their knees. Headlines proclaimed the good news:

City's Biggest Church Packed Twice Daily for Prayer
—New Haven, Connecticut

Business Shuts Down for Hour Each Day; Everybody Prays
—Bethel, Connecticut

State Legislators Get Down on Knees
—Albany, New York

Ice on the Mohawk Broken for Baptisms
—Schenectady, New York

Five Prayer Meetings Go Round the Clock
—Washington, D.C.

Revival Sweeps Yale
—New Haven, Connecticut[17]

The Great Prayer Revival of 1857–1859, like the First and Second Great Awakenings, was unique. Unlike either movement before it, the revival Lanphier sparked was almost totally led by laypersons, began and flourished throughout all denominations, and relied on united prayer. Yet despite all their uniqueness, look at what all three Great Awakenings show us about revival. We can't predict it. We can't plan it. We can't shape it.

We can only trust that when our nation reaches a point of spiritual, moral, and social no-return—as it appeared to do at least three distinct times in history—an extraordinary movement of God's Spirit may move in extraordinary ways in response to prayer for God's broken, contrite children. Every time God has moved in such a way in our country, He has done so through the simple confession, brokenness, and obedience of individuals. This is totally consistent with how God always seems to bring His people back to Himself. Might He do it again in this Jesus-Now Awakening!

Walking in the Light of God's Word

Then Jesus said to those Jews who believed Him, "If you abide in My word, you are My disciples indeed. And you shall know the truth, and the truth shall make you free." (John 8:31–32)

In John 8:31–59, Jesus offers encounters with His Word as a means to deepened transformation in Christ-likeness. Encountering Jesus in the Word transforms us into His likeness, empowering our testimony of revival and awakening.

- Truth cannot be subjectively created; truth is and comes from the objective, absolute person of Christ. As John wrote: "For the law was given through Moses, *but* grace and truth came through Jesus Christ" (John 1:17).

- Truth cannot be relative and change from person to person, from community to community, because Jesus is the incarnation of the God who "with whom there is no variation or shifting shadow" (James 1:17 NASB). As the Scripture says: "Jesus Christ *is* the same yesterday, today, and forever" (Hebrews 13:8).

- All proclaimed truth cannot be equal because Jesus didn't claim to be "a truth," one that is equal to all others. His claim was exclusive. He claimed to be the one and only truth, the only way to God. "Jesus said to him, 'I am the way, the truth, and the life. No one comes to the Father except through Me' " (John 14:6). Those are not the words of someone who is "one among many," someone who is "equal" to all others; those are the words of One who has no equal.

"I am the LORD, and there is no other; *There is* no God besides Me. I will gird you, though you have not known Me, that they may know from the rising of the sun to its setting that *there is* none besides Me. I *am* the LORD, and *there is* no other" (Isaiah 45:5–6).

Living our conviction to be pleasing to Jesus, at all costs, means we live a unique and Spirit-led life even as we champion Jesus as our exclusive hope.

Pause and reflect on areas of your life that have potential for growth and change as you embrace specific truth from Scripture. Where could spiritual awakening take place in your life as you walk in the light of God's Word? How might this better empower your missional living?

Dear Lord, please search me thoroughly and help me to become aware of the areas that are hindering my spiritual maturity and witness. What truth from the Word do you want me to embrace, so that I might experience more of your freedom and better express Jesus?

Speak to me, Lord. your servant is listening...

M-3 Championing Jesus as the only hope of eternal life and abundant living

REVIVAL IN JUDAH

The story of King Hezekiah provides a clear, biblical example of how revival blesses a nation through the faithfulness of one person. Seven hundred years before the birth of Christ may seem light years away from today—until you read Hezekiah's description of his society. "For our fathers have trespassed and done evil in the eyes of the LORD our God; they have forsaken Him, have turned their faces away from the dwelling place of the LORD, and turned *their* backs *on Him*" (2 Chronicles 29:6).

Yet through the faith of one man, King Hezekiah, their long march of disobedience and drought ended. (Imagine reclaiming your own house of worship after it had been condemned by years of indifference and spiritual decay.)

Through the vision, courage, and faith of one person, a nation began to return to God. The call of Hezekiah resulted in a revival in which "all the assembly worshiped, the singers sang, and the trumpeters sounded; all *this continued* until the burnt offering was finished" (2 Chronicles 29:28).

Worship was just the beginning. Something truly remarkable happened that had not taken place in generations; believers called upon each other to repent (2 Chronicles 30:6). The call brought new unity (30:12) and a new desire among the people to give a greater portion of their earthly treasures back to God (2 Chronicles 31:12). Individual renewal grew into a tremendous corporate response as people shared their material possessions with others in need (31:19). What began as humble confession became a movement of national repentance, obedience, and meaningful social change.

This is exactly what happened in each of our country's Great Awakenings. When a nation's darkness becomes overwhelmingly destructive, only God can supply what people need to be brought back to life. These things include the assurance of being forgiven, accepted, and loved; the joy of worshiping God alone; and a return to holy living. When God brings revival to a nation, He blesses His people with a call to return to six specific commitments:

1. Authority of the Scripture
2. Belief in the centrality of the cross of Jesus
3. Increased devotional life and return to personal holiness

4. Renewed spiritual authority of biblical preaching from the pulpit
5. Explosive witnessing and discipleship
6. Corporate social change that results from individual, spiritual transformation

Does seeing the embryonic development of one or more of these things mean our nation is one step closer to revival?

In my view, this is the wrong question to ask. Trying to predict any movement of God's Spirit is impossible and even harmful. We could be so absorbed in wanting to know, "When will it happen?" that we lose an appreciation for how consistent God's expression of love is in revival. The great thing about seeing how God has revived our nation three times in our history (and how He revived His covenant people in Scripture) is that we see God's consistent character and blessing at work.

Though the means of each revival were unique to each time, people, and place, God's results were resoundingly clear. The attraction of these timeless results isn't that they help us *predict* revival (they can't), but rather that they cause us to *long* to fast and pray for revival. When you see what marvelous things God has done through revival, you can't help but ask, "What if?"

What if God were to move through our land in a way that caused people to admit they could no longer go on with their broken, unhappy lives?

What if people turned from their self-centered greed, corruption, prejudice, hatred, and violence?

What if the change was so obvious, so far beyond explanation, that people everywhere freely announced, "This could only come from God!"?

Imagine what would happen if true revival visited our nation once more:

- People would love one another with God's love in their thoughts, desires, and, most of all, their actions!
- The Bible would return to company boardrooms, schools, legislative halls, and homes of people who know it's *the* authoritative source for living.
- A new understanding of the cross of Jesus Christ would sweep the land. People would relearn how much we deserved to die, what Christ did in our place, and the value of the resurrection.
- Widespread prayer and worship would be embraced by people who bring to their workplaces, classrooms, and homes a kind of love that makes people put away their mistrust, fear, and dislike for one another.
- Christians would freely and openly share Jesus with people who not only accept Christ but hunger to know God through an amazing resurgence of study and prayer.
- Cities and towns would be transformed by group after group of Christians, causing an astounded public to admit, "Never has this city seen such compassion and love that truly works."
- Church pulpits would resound with the truth of God's Word.

It's ironic that the man who reconfirmed these realities in the midst of America's Second Great Awakening was a legendary evangelist, who believed there was nothing miraculous about revival and that spiritual awakening was not so much God's intervention but the inevitable, unquestioned result of people's obedience. Though rationalism was the enemy of faith, it's interesting that Charles Finney used his God-given gifts of rational insight and reasoning to communicate the need for revival.

CHARLES FINNEY:
"WHAT WILL YOU DO WITH JESUS CHRIST?"

Charles Finney was born in 1792 and reared with little Christian influence. As a young student of law in Adams, New York, he attended church and even sang in the choir as an unbeliever to improve his law practice. Yet, since so much of law in his day was based upon Scripture, Finney was forced to consult the Bible on a regular basis. This tall, angular member of the New York Bar Association made sure his reference Bible was hidden under other books on his desk so that others wouldn't see it. Before the concept of revival ever entered his mind—while he debated with himself whether to give his life to God—the authority of Scripture became all too real. Walking back to his office one autumn day, Finney heard a voice he could not deny: "Will you accept it now, today?" After moments of soul searching, Finney remembered the words of Scripture: "Then shall ye see me and find me, when ye shall search for me with all your heart." He cried out, "Lord, I take Thee at Thy Word."[18]

The authority of Scripture and the conviction that sin could be eradicated in a person's life only through the cross and the resurrection of Jesus Christ—the very things he would one day preach to thousands—changed Finney's life. He described his dramatic moment of conversion "like a wave of electricity going through me … I could not express it in any other way. It seemed like the very breath of God."[19]

Wherever Finney preached throughout western New York, crowds came. Almost always, true revival was the result. Almost without exception, people who heard Finney's sermons began confessing their sins, repenting, and weeping. During one historic, six-month preaching tour in Rochester, New York, a hundred thousand people gave their lives to Christ. In Boston, fifty thousand decisions were counted during the week Finney preached. Once when Finney was speaking in Philadelphia, a group of lumbermen, who heard him and responded, returned as spiritual ambassadors to the woods where no schools, churches, or pastors existed. During the next year, five thousand people in their community came to Christ.

Many disagreed with Finney's personal preaching style. While most preachers talked about "the sins of others," Finney addressed his audiences directly. "What will you do with Jesus Christ?" Finney always demanded a verdict on this all-important issue. Many of those converted began to exert a profound social impact in their day.[20]

Like Hezekiah before him and Lanphier to follow, Finney saw the mark of true revival: Christians with the power to change society because their inner beings had changed. Their actions were the overflow of God's undeniable love, which they could no longer keep to themselves, magnetically attracting others to Jesus.

FINNEY'S "SEVEN INDICATORS"

Charles Finney couldn't know at the time that he was living in the last period of spiritual awakening our country has seen until now. How ironic that he would write his "Seven Indicators" of coming revival. He used his brilliant human intellect to help us understand how God's infinite Holy Spirit breathes life into a nation. Finney was not interested in forecasting history, yet—approximately two hundred years after they were written—Finney's indicators may cause us to think again about extraordinary expressions of the Holy Spirit in our nation that have already caused many to say, "I had no idea these things were happening."

How many Americans, today, do you think believe our country is ripe for revival, if not already experiencing a new great awakening? What would they—what would *you*—say in light of Finney's "Seven Indicators"?

1. When the sovereignty of God indicates that revival is near
2. When wickedness grieves and humbles Christians
3. Where there is a spirit of prayer for revival
4. When the attention of ministers is directed toward revival and spiritual awakening
5. When Christians confess their sins one to another
6. When Christians are willing to make the sacrifices necessary to carry out the new movement of God's Spirit
7. When the ministers and laity are willing for God to promote spiritual awakening by whatever instrument he pleases[21]

How many of these seven indicators would you say are real and present where you live and worship? One? Two? Five? How many have you already seen reported in the newspaper or heard about from a friend in church? Let's take a closer look at several of these seven indicators.

Franklin Graham, son of the heralded evangelist Billy Graham, writes:

Hardly a day passes that I don't hear someone say, "We are losing our country; we are losing our churches."

While doomsday appears to be knocking at our door, let me take you back to the early 1800s. Many think of it as "the good old days," but history tells us that society, even then, was as bad as it could get at that time. John Marshall, chief justice of the United States Supreme Court, wrote to President James Madison and said, "The church is too far gone ever to be redeemed." When we examine why, we find that preachers had stopped preaching the whole Gospel of Jesus Christ, and the people were not hearing God's Word.

What changed? Christians began to diligently pray for revival—and the result was the Second Great Awakening. When people's prayers stormed the heavens, and when the Bible was opened in the pulpits and the Word of God proclaimed by passionate preachers, the church was awakened from slumber by the Holy Spirit, who moved in hearts, spreading revival throughout the heartland of America.

There have been several Great Awakenings in our nation's history. When I read about them, I always go back to the Old Testament, to a time in which Israel had once again turned its back on God. When its people came to their senses, they gathered and asked Ezra the scribe to bring the Word of the Lord to them. The Bible tells us that Ezra stood upon a pulpit of wood, and he opened the book in the sight of all the people (Nehemiah 8).

Prayer is the key to reaching lost people for Christ, and I hope you will begin praying now for neighbors, co-workers, friends, and family who do not know Jesus Christ as Savior. Make a point to pray for your church and other churches in your community, asking God to stir up an ever-increasing urgency for evangelism.[22]

Billy Graham's "Prayer for the Nation" is a call for pastors and all ministers of the gospel (as well as all Americans) to confess their individual sins, as well as the collective sin of our country:

Our Father and Our God, we praise You for Your goodness to our nation, giving us blessings far beyond what we deserve. Yet we know all is not right with America. We deeply need a moral and spiritual renewal to help us meet the many problems we face. Convict us of sin. Help us to turn to You in repentance and faith. Set our feet on the path of Your righteousness and peace. We pray today for our nation's leaders. Give them the wisdom to know what is right, and the courage to do it. You have said, "Blessed is the nation whose God is the Lord." May this be a new era for America, as we humble ourselves and acknowledge You alone as our Savior and Lord? This we pray in Your holy name, Amen.[23]

NEW DAY DAWNING

Finney's observations are worth examining because they point to personal revival of Christians in pockets of our country.

If a Jesus-Now Awakening is dawning in America, I believe I may already have caught a glimpse of what it looks like in the stories of many other Jesus followers across our nation. If a Fifth Great Awakening is yet to come, it may look like what has already begun to unfold in Portland, Oregon; Long Island, New York; and Memphis, Tennessee. The more I've listened to people tell their still-unfolding stories, the more I've become intrigued by the striking similarities of our nation's past and present-day turbulence.

Should the gatherings of public confession and corporate prayer in churches across our country be called merely isolated events? Or is something greater happening? Is this "something else" a new, dramatic unfolding of God's Jesus-Now plan?

The only way to know is to sit back and listen to the stories, seeing His work in others with the eyes of a man or woman of Issachar. And let the evidence speak for itself.

Walking in the Light of God's People

**He who has My commandments and keeps them,
it is he who loves Me. (John 14:21)**

A life of Jesus-Now revival is expressed through passionate love of the Lord and as His Word is lived out with people in freedom and boldness. Reflect on a recent time when you have lived out His Word:

- Romans 15:7 — *I recently expressed Christ-like acceptance to____ when …*

- Proverbs 15:1 — *I shared a gentle response in the face of anger when …*

- James 5:16 — *I recently apologized to _____ concerning …*

- Romans 12:15 — *I was able to rejoice with _____ over …*

- Romans 12:15 — *I was able to mourn with _____ over …*

Allow the Holy Spirit to ask you often: "What Bible verses did you experience today?"

**W-8 Living "naturally supernatural"
in all of life as His Spirit makes the written Word, the living Word**

SPIRIT-EMPOWERED
Faith

FOUR

Pockets of Light Shining out of Darkness

The room was filled with approximately one hundred pastors from every major denomination and independent group throughout the Pacific Northwest. They had gathered for training before a Billy Graham Evangelistic Crusade.

I stood before the group that morning and began my talk with a question.

"How many of you in this room are praying for revival, for spiritual awakening in your area of North America, for an extraordinary movement of God's Spirit to sweep through your church?"

No more than six or seven people raised their hands.

"How many of you are praying on a consistent basis? How many of you, when you look at your church and look at our nation, are seeing signs of revival—brokenness, confession, and prayer that could only come from God?"

Practically no hands went up.

That was May 1983. For the next several years, I found this "no hands" response the same in the United States and around the world. If people were praying for revival, they weren't talking about it or admitting it, at least to me.

Eight years later in February 1991, I stood before a similar group of church leaders in the same city, preparing for another Billy Graham Crusade. "For the past twenty years, as an organizer of evangelistic crusades, I've visited with church and lay leaders in almost every region of the country," I said. "Everywhere I've gone, I've asked people a question, the same one I'd like to ask you: "How many of you here this morning are praying for revival, a spiritual awakening in our nation?"

WILL YOU NOT REVIVE US AGAIN?

The words of the psalmist, who is hungry for revival, still resonate in our hearts today: "Will You not revive us again, that Your people may rejoice in You?" (Psalm 85:6). Much like previous revivals, the emerging Jesus-Now Awakening resists definition.

Similar to a pinprick of light in an ever-darkening, national mood, God's small yet brilliant presence has pierced through unexpectedly. Many have yet to see it. Like the cave Clay and I explored, prolonged darkness can seem to block out light. The daily onslaught of war, road rage, and moral decay numbs and blinds us to see God's hand of blessing. Some have wandered away, and remained distant, from God for so long they've stopped seeking the Light of the World, Jesus Christ.

Others, however, have a different story to tell. Their testimonies can open our spiritual eyes to see how God is awakening our nation:

- Pastors in Philadelphia are pursuing radical reconciliation.
- America's youth are returning to sexual purity.
- Scores of men are confessing to each other that they've not been the kind of husbands and fathers God desires.

These are a few of the many "pockets of light" where Jesus, the Light of the World, is increasingly shining. The illumination is growing both nationally and internationally.

I'm one of the increasing numbers of Christians in our land who believe the infancy of this Jesus-Now Awakening is for real. I celebrate all that God is now doing with a healthy smidgen of caution for the church. In seeing the first signs of spiritual awakening, we think we've seen it all. It's tempting to think, "This *must* be revival because the fresh, new love for Jesus matches up with spiritual awakenings of the nation's past." Human nature wants to label, organize, package, and distribute spiritual truth. (Even this book is an attempt to provide "handles" to grasp the awesome wonder of Jesus, who is so much greater than any words can begin to describe.)

Familiarizing ourselves with historic revivals can raise our anticipation to welcome in the present great awakening. Knowing how God has uniquely worked in the past can prepare us to receive and bless the One who revives us for His glory and praise. "Will You not revive us again, that Your people may rejoice in You?" (Psalm 85:6). The heart of revival is, of course, the Lord making His heart one with ours. "Draw near to God and He will draw near to you" (James 4:8).

Walking
in the Light
of God's
Son

But God demonstrates His own love toward us, in that while we
were still sinners, Christ died for us. (Romans 5:8 NASB)

God declared our infinite, unconditional worth at Calvary. Pause to allow His Spirit to overwhelm you with the wonder of His love—unmerited, unstoppable, and unlimited. Give Him thanks. His Spirit desires to empower your expression of this same love one to another. The testimony of the gospel is that your true identity is not determined by what you do. You and I could do nothing to merit being made part of His family. Pause to give our Savior praise and worship.

Lord Jesus, as I reflect on your unmerited, undeserved love toward me, my heart is moved with ...

L-4 Regularly rejoicing in my identity as "His beloved"

GOD AT THE CENTER

The only way to approach and participate in the imminent great awakening is to keep in mind it is all about God and God alone. "I will praise You, O Lord my God, with all my heart, and I will glorify Your name forevermore" (Psalm 86:12). Everything having to do with revival throughout our nation's history, as well as today, centers on God's nature and God's purposes revealed in His Word.

During the past two decades, the growing prevalence of ungodliness in our country has actually heightened a new readiness and hunger for God. For those who have spiritual eyes to see, the powers of darkness and light have become almost inescapable. Like the cave that I wandered into as a teen, the destructive forces in our world seem overpowering and ready to swallow us up. Yet the truth is God's light has never been extinguished, and for good reason: "For it is the God who commanded light to shine out of darkness, who has shone in our hearts to give the light of the knowledge of the glory of God in the face of Jesus Christ" (2 Corinthians 4:6). Today, God's light is shining in the hearts of Jesus' followers in some of the darkest corners of our nation and our world.

In 2013, Chanda Crout, a wife and mother in Gilbert, South Carolina, felt stirred to pray. She and her husband had served the previous two years in Tegbi, Ghana (West Africa), with Father's House International, a ministry that rescues children out of slavery. "As in-country directors, we gave eight boys a new home where they were safe. We were their parents and taught them about Jesus, so they could experience His love, learn to trust Him and discover the Lord's hope and purpose for their lives," Chanda shared.

Once home in South Carolina, Chanda confronted a dark, disturbing chapter in her state's heritage. "It's a history of rebellion and greed, including years of slavery involving tobacco and others crops. I felt a strong call to confess the sins of our state, our people, and our government. I didn't fully understand it at the time, but I knew I had to seek the Lord in a deep spirit of repentance and ask Him to plant new seeds of obedience among our people. The Lord was directing me to seek out, meet, and pray with our governor, Nicky Haley."

True to her conviction, Chanda traveled to the South Carolina State House in Columbia. "I prayed that the Lord would direct my path to the governor's office. The first thing I saw when I arrived on the grounds was a monument to African-Americans. In the granite stone, amazingly, I saw an image of the country of Ghana and arrows pointing to South Carolina.

"In that moment, it all came together for me. If we are going to see a spiritual awakening of God, we need, *I need*, to repent from our past sins. I heard the Lord say, 'I have allowed you to see this monument and see the connection of slavery and of sin between Ghana and South Carolina because I am a God of redemption. I want you to see the redemptive work in Ghana and the redemptive work I am doing in South Carolina.'

"I was simply awestruck. I began to repent for myself, my

family, and the leaders of my state." Soon, Chanda was face-to-face with Governor Nikki Haley. "After some brief conversation in her office, I asked if she would be willing to pray with me. Governor Haley extended her hand and bowed her head. I thanked God for her life and her position in government. I asked God to guard her and surround her so that He would be glorified. I prayed that the people of our state—our businesses, schools, churches, and leaders—would repent and receive the Lord's forgiveness."

God is transforming corners of darkness into new pockets of light and life in places like South Carolina. Two things have happened: (1) people who had been surrounded, and thus lost, in spiritual darkness have been awakened, and (2) they have been drawn to the light outside of their cave.

Jesus, who brings light to God's human creation (John 1:4), is turning the corners of darkness in our cities, workplaces, schools, and churches into new pockets of light. Those who see and surrender to Jesus are being awakened to God, who was there all along. In the life and light of Jesus, they're basking in the freeing truth that revival comes not from our own determination but rather from *God's* initiation—in *His* timing and for *His* purposes.

Walking
in the Light
of God's
Word

To the praise of the glory of His grace. (Ephesians 1:6 NASB)

Pause to reflect on your experience of the glory of God's grace, recently or in the past. Be still before the Lord and ask His Spirit to stir memories, perhaps of times when …

- He unexpectedly provided for you.
- He pursued and accepted you in the midst of a failure.

- He supported you in your physical or emotional pain.
- He restored a broken relationship.

Complete the following sentence:

I give thanks and praise to God for the grace He gave me when ...

W-2 Being a living epistle in reverence and awe as His Word becomes real in my life

"AND MY WILL BE LOST IN THINE"

Today, as more followers of Jesus are drawn to the same light, another truth becomes apparent: Revival reveals God's distinctive calling to fulfill His purposes for each generation.

Pick up a leading news magazine or read through the national news section of your daily paper, and you're bound to read about one or more Christian leaders and their respective ministries making news:

- Daniel Kolenda is one of thirty-three Christian leaders under thirty-three years of age, recognized by *Christianity Today*. Kolenda, a missionary and open-air evangelist, has purportedly led millions to Christ. He is a fifth-generation preacher whose ministry is marked by a powerful evangelistic anointing (preaching, teaching, and healing). Most importantly, the poor have the gospel preached to them. It is this single-minded, gospel emphasis that makes the ministry of Daniel Kolenda and Christ for All Nations so unique.

- Jefferson Bethke's rhythmic, spoken-word, "Why I Hate Religion but Love Jesus," long-since went viral on YouTube. Bethke's raw, rapid-fire delivery has been fresh kindling to stoke new interest in the gospel, especially among youth. According to *The Christian Post's* website, one contributor to Bethke's Facebook wall wrote, "Your poem helped me remember that the church is a place for the broken," while another revealed that she was giving herself to God, realizing that He could love her despite her past.

  "Let's never forget to preach the gospel of grace!" Bethke encouraged on his wall. "Get out of the way, make Jesus famous, and watch people be transformed. He is good!"[1]

  Kolenda and Bethke are inspiring examples of Jesus' loving, redemptive heart beating inside His beloved children. The outward work of revival grows out of God's distinctive calling to fulfill His purposes for each generation.

- Campus Renewal Ministries, led by Jeremy Story, is seeing college campuses transformed across the nation as next generation followers join this Jesus-Now Awakening. Catalyzing united movements for Christ is the vision of Campus Renewal. They live this vision as students, campus ministries, and local churches come together in prayer and evangelism.

- The Convergence Movement, led by pastors Corey and Jade Lee, is making an incredible impact in the inner city of Atlanta, Georgia. Convergence is launching generational influencers from campuses to inner cities and from inner cities to the ends of the earth.

They're doing this by harnessing the power of the emerging generation and by modeling and establishing healthy relationships.

From Hezekiah forward, revival has not depended upon one's leadership ability but rather on God's grace to involve His humble, obedient followers. "Humble yourselves in the sight of the Lord, and He will lift you up" (James 4:10).

- George Whitefield preached with passion and theatrical flair, yet the First Great Awakening did not rest on his sermons.
- Jeremiah Lanphier was a faithful prayer warrior and promoter, yet the thousands who eventually came to Christ didn't do so because they were impressed by Lanphier.
- Fanny Crosby wrote scores of inspiring hymns, yet the millions of Sunday worshipers weren't directing their praise to her as they sang:

Consecrate me now to Thy service, Lord,
By the power of grace divine;
Let my soul look up with a steadfast hope,
And my will be lost in Thine.[2]

God does not allow any person, or their followers, to take credit for the extraordinary work and results God alone can accomplish through His Holy Spirit. Anyone God is using to advance the current spiritual awakening understands this.

They lift up the name of Jesus because Jesus, alone, lives in them. Therefore, they have no need or reason to control, shape, and mold what they see as "their ministry." Instead, they accurately and humbly recognize that true ministry honors God. They don't long to be in the limelight. Like John the Baptist, everything about their lives points to Jesus, the Light of the World.

For years, I've searched for a way to grasp and convey this truth. Whenever I've tried to explain it, the result has been preaching more than teaching. One day I spoke to a small group of church leaders who began the meeting by voicing their doubts that spiritual awakening was even possible in our time. Since I didn't know these men and women (and they surely didn't know me), I decided to put their skepticisms to the side and tell them a little bit about who I was. That's when I found my illustration for revival. The analogy I had been seeking for years was part of my own story.

A LAND RIPE FOR REVIVAL

I grew up on a farm, homesteaded by my grandfather, Joseph Whitefield Phillips, in northeastern Mississippi. This Primitive Baptist circuit rider with a revivalist middle name had built a large home out of sandstone rocks. It was perched on a bluff and looked out on rolling fields where cotton, soybeans, and corn grew. As a small boy, I could stand on the front porch and watch as combines and tractors crawled through the scorching heat with my uncles and older cousins at the wheel. I could always tell by the looks on their faces and by the conversation over dinner if it had been a good harvest. But I never understood the full meaning of what was at stake in the autumn months that followed. When the days grew shorter and darker, I came to see the meaning of the harvest.

Every fall, it happened. After the cotton, corn, and soybeans were picked, the stalks and the leftover vegetation would be turned under. The dry soil that summer had turned into hard clods was dissolved by tractor disks. When the breaking was complete, the earth became finer than cornmeal. Fertilizing occurred in the early spring, then planting in April or May.

In the late spring, I could see my Uncle Millard standing in a sea of dark brown earth that held our family's future. Against an orange sky at dusk, his weather-beaten body made a striking silhouette. I would see him stoop over, pick up a handful of moist, cool soil, and let it run through his hands. Then he would look up, and I knew what he was saying, "God, we've done all that we can do, and now this crop is in your hands. The ground is tilled. The fertilizer is there. The seeds are in the ground. We can't touch them until they grow. Only with the rain and sun you bring will we see new life."

This picture captures my own living analogy for the time of spiritual awakening that awaits our nation. For years, our country, our land, has produced a bountiful spiritual harvest through believers who, like sprouting seeds, have lived the normal Christian life. They have fulfilled their purpose and died so that new life could grow.

The "harvests," in which people such as George Whitefield, Jeremiah Lanphier, and Charles Finney participated, revived a dead land, not permanently, but for a season of years. In extraordinary seasons of awakening the Lord has seen fit to rain down His Holy Spirit, and humble people have admitted to God, "We've done all that we can do. Lord, we are in your hands."

From most outward appearances today, many would doubt that another extraordinary spiritual harvest could come from the land we call home. There are too many weeds. There has been too much drought. And there's a desperate shortage of caring workers. Yet even these things cannot deny a fact that is now coming to the surface. America is experiencing two distinct "harvests."

One is a harvest of seed that has never known the ground of truth. Without the right and natural place in which to grow, without the surrounding "nutrients" of Scripture, the "seeds" (people) have sprouted unsatisfying roots that have nowhere to go. America is filled with such seeds of God's creation, people who sink their roots into dark places where soil and sunlight are non-existent. Instead of maturing into the creation God intended, they grow according to their uprooted condition. Instead of soil, they seek unhealthy substitutes—destructive chemicals (alcohol and drugs), unnatural, destructive influences (promiscuity, homosexuality, abortion), and the wrong balance of God-given elements (money, people, and possessions). Seeds allowed to rot prove the truth of The Agronomist's Law: "No root, no shoot, no fruit."

This ungodly crop of America is the "harvest" of a people who have never known God's true ground of the Holy Spirit, the Bible, and the church. It's no coincidence this "harvest" emerged in the early 1960s as municipal, state, and federal laws regulated the Bible and prayer out of public schools. The result is that millions of baby boomers from this era, along with their offspring, will never mature spiritually to be all that God truly intends unless they discover a true, growing environment where America's other harvest is silently waiting to bloom.

Except, one element is missing.

For at least the past half-century, our nation has been suffering a spiritual drought. Ever since the end of World War II, our churches, our schools, and our families have often failed to sink their roots into healthy soil. During this time, the guiding truth of God's Word has lost ground to individually minded values. As self-centered desires have eroded God-centered principles and relationships, our people have grown up less and less fulfilled. In the meantime, something else has happened. The land has become arid.

For whatever reason, over the last twenty or thirty years, the rain of the Holy Spirit has been increasingly absent across our land. Many Christians have felt this drought; many churches have experienced it. Yet, the fact is many "good seeds" have found a home in the healthy, growing ground of Christ-centered churches, small groups, and one-to-one relationships. These pockets of believers remind me of how soybean seeds can exist for months in soil without rain. These are the people who are ready for the Holy Spirit to rain down—the people ready to come alive. They are the people ripe for revival.

In one way, the seed that's rotting away and the seed that's ready to awaken from the ground are strangely alike. Each can go no further and grow no further without outside help. In the context of today's revival stirrings, you and I are like the farmer who admits, "I've done all that I possibly can, Lord. Now, you must bring the rain."

Look what is already happening! Sprinkled across our nation, God's early rains have begun to fall. On our youth. On men. On women. On pastors, who know what true brokenness, confession, and repentance are all about—and who know God is doing something extraordinary in them and through them.

In specific areas of our country, on specific groups of broken, humbled people, God's Holy Spirit is beginning to lightly rain. Previous revivals have known this same, refreshing Spirit. Yet what's happening today is unique from anything our country has ever experienced and uniquely personal to every life He's touching. Would you prayerfully consider how you might be a part of this Jesus-Now Awakening?

A SQUIRT OF TABASCO SAUCE

Planted next to the tallest high-rise in downtown Vancouver, British Columbia, is a relatively small brick building, called Coastal Church. In a city where only 3 percent make time for Sunday worship, approximately 2,000 people, representing eighty nationalities, pack into the pews.

"We've become a home to so many ethnicities that we've run

out of flags," says senior pastor David Koop. "Revival is taking place in our midst. Every evening, 200 seekers and newcomers to faith, line up for Alpha classes."

David Koop and his wife, Cheryl, befriended me at a conference in Vancouver, where we experienced good conversation, worship, and prayer. I can tell you, everything I've written about spiritual awakening in this book points to the fresh, sweet, and spicy scent of God's Spirit at Coastal Church. As a dear, trusted Anglican friend of David's described the Coastal Church to him, "You're a Baptist church with Tabasco Sauce."

Says Koop, "Our passion is to re-take the heart of the city, where 89 percent of our resident-neighbors are in their twenties and thirties, 61 percent live alone, and 66 percent eat meals by themselves. It's not surprising that the number one need in our city, confirmed by rigorous, revealing research, is loneliness. Loneliness and the feeling of being unwanted is the most terrible poverty. To that end, we at Coastal Church haven't really even begun to reach the lost."

"One of the hardest things we faced," says David, "was to work with Vancouver city officials to put up a cross in front of our church. Because of the cross of Jesus Christ, we knew we could approach God in confidence and pray in the name and authority of Jesus Christ for His will to be done. All of us will never forget the day when we planted a beautiful, ten-foot wooden cross in the ground a few feet from the busy sidewalk on West George Street in downtown Vancouver."

Koop goes on, "Everyone who walks by, waits for a bus, or scurries to work is confronted with Jesus Christ and what took place on *His* cross. It really presents the gospel at eye level. None of the revival we're experiencing at Coastal Church would have happened without continual surrender, fasting, and prayer before the Lord. Fasting and prayer is where our life in Jesus Christ begins."

What unites these individuals is God bringing His people together on their knees. For them, and for you, true spiritual awakening rests with one act of humility and reverence before God—prayer.

"Prayer," said the late evangelist, pastor, and author R.A. Torrey, "is the key that unlocks all the storehouses of God's infinite grace and power. All that God is, and all that God has, is at the disposal of prayer."

What the Bible teaches, what Charles Finney suggests, and what Christians about whom you've read are committed, is the one element that will bring us face-to-face with God. That one element, the key to the new Great Awakening in North America and personal revival, is prayer.

Walking
in the Light
of God's
People

For without Me you can do nothing. (John 15:5)

None of us, in our own strength, has any hope of living an abundant life. It's only persistent, prevailing prayer that is our open doorway into this Jesus-Now Awakening.

Pray with one or two other people, making this declaration of helplessness:

Lord, my power and strength are insufficient. I need you to involve me in all that you are up to.

Pray this prayer of humility with other people. Believe together that Jesus is present, sufficient, and available.

P-10 Humbly acknowledging to the Lord, ourselves, and others that it is Jesus in and through us who loves others at their point of need

SPIRIT-
EMPOWERED
Faith

FIVE

Prayer:
The Heartbeat of Revival

On September 12, 1990, forty-five thousand junior and senior high students from a handful of states around the US gathered in circles around the flagpoles of their respective schools to pray for God's presence, strength, and direction in their classrooms, homes, cities, and towns. The "See You at the Pole" gathering swelled to one million students the following year. By 2014, this unprecedented day of student-led prayer involved three million followers of Jesus in twenty countries. As in all great movements of prayer, "See You at the Pole" did not begin in the hearts of people but rather in the heart of God. God used the obedience of a small group of teens to ignite what has become an international movement of prayer among young people.

THE HABIT OF PRAYER

Almost twenty-five years ago, I couldn't fully understand how prayer would prepare me for the new spiritual awakening, unfolding today. In January 1991, I was directing the Washington State Billy Graham Crusade in the Seattle-Tacoma area. The logistical challenges were unprecedented and enormous. We had only four months lead time, just one-third of the time needed to plan most crusades. This was a unique Crusade in Mr. Graham's ministry because it would be held back-to-back in two major indoor, domed stadiums—the Tacoma Dome and the Kingdome in Seattle. Yet, another "first," one of great, spiritual significance, shed new light on the need for prayer to *further the spiritual awakening God is bringing about in our day.*

Early in the Crusade's planning stages, several prayer intercessors in the Seattle-Tacoma area said they especially wanted to move into the Tacoma Dome and the Kingdome sites to fast and pray for the Crusade's evangelistic meetings as the events took place. To my knowledge, it was the first time in forty years of Billy Graham Crusade meetings that local residents had volunteered to actually reside in the Crusade's stadia from the time the site was first arranged to fast and pray in an organized effort.

Naturally, I was totally supportive. As many as eighty people began to fast and pray one to two hours a day, some during free time at their jobs, others at home. Some people prayed as many as eight hours a day. These dedicated prayer warriors said, "We want to pray at the stadium. We want to pray for the stadium, the workers, and all the people who will be part of the meetings." Though the stadium officials told us there were laws against anyone residing on the premises, they agreed to let Crusade volunteers use two rooms. I suspected these stadium officials perceived the Crusade as just another event. Yet I sensed they saw the value of prayer. I detected they knew that they and their fellow workers needed prayer. So, they graciously agreed to allow Crusade volunteers to come and pray for the several days they had requested.

The first major gathering was held on Thursday night, April 3, at the Tacoma Dome. The stadium was packed to capacity even though the Seattle-Tacoma region received a record rainfall. The deluge that flooded the freeways caused Mr. Graham to say, somewhat tongue-in-cheek, "I thought I should preach on Noah's ark!"

In a room beneath the bleachers, a group of more than eighty men and women gathered to intercede in prayer and ask God's protection and direction for the meeting. During the prayer time, one person shared: "As I've been praying, I'm seeing black and white figures. Not that some are black and others are white. These figures are both black and white. They're evil. We need to pray against them." No one in the room could understand what this was about, yet the group began to pray against these unknown images.

Three days later on Sunday afternoon, I was confirming last-minute details at the Kingdome for the final evangelistic meeting of the Crusade. The chief security officer found me and said, "We've got a problem. Some gay activists are out in front of the stadium, passing out condoms." The official explained that since the protest conflicted with our purposes, and since we had rented the facility, he had authority to ask them to leave.

"There's another problem, though," he said. "They want to come inside the Kingdome."

"As a matter of security, what do you think about that?" I asked him.

"Well," he said, "if they come in, they'll have to take off their habits. You see, they're dressed like nuns. They're all in black and white."

God had already shown the intercessors to pray against an organized onslaught that we couldn't see, but that He knew was coming. The antagonists were welcomed inside the Kingdome where they gathered with the pray-ers and heard the saving message of God's love in Jesus.

All my life I had believed that God worked through prayer to mend broken relationships, heal emotional and physical wounds, and make "the impossible" real for His glory, but this was different. As I traveled to different cities throughout the United States, I sensed something wonderful and historic with prayer was already occurring.

As I talked to church leaders and lay persons, as I listened and observed, meditated, and prayed, I kept coming back to Charles Finney, the great revivalist of the nineteenth century. Though they were 130 years old, Finney's "Seven Indicators" of spiritual awakening were fresh in my mind. As you recall from chapter three, Finney believed revival would come when:

1. The sovereignty of God indicates that revival is near.
2. Wickedness grieves and humbles Christians.
3. There is a spirit of prayer for revival.
4. The attention of ministers is directed toward revival and spiritual awakening.
5. Christians confess their sins one to another.
6. Christians are willing to make the sacrifices necessary to carry out the new movement of God's Spirit.
7. The ministers and laity are willing for God to promote spiritual awakening by whatever instrument he pleases.[1]

I will be the first to admit that the Jesus-Now Awakening cannot be confirmed by one man's list of characteristics. I don't know if Finney was accurate in all that he said. I'm not convinced that each of the seven indicators needs to be operative. However, all of the seven except for one had begun to surface. Listen prayerfully as God seeks to enlist you in this Jesus-Now Awakening.

Walking
in the Light
of God's
Word

I pray that the eyes of your heart may be enlightened in order that you may know the hope to which he has called you. (Ephesians 1:18 NIV)

Plan to pause and pray together with another person. Claim the promise of Ephesians 1:18 that we might see and hear as Jesus does. Just as the Scripture notes that Abraham was a "friend of God," rejoice together that you also are the friend of God and He longs to reveal Himself to you and involve you in His kingdom purposes. God wants to confide in you and then co-labor with you for His eternal glory. Ask Him to bless the fruitfulness of the work He has called you to do in this Jesus-Now Awakening.

> *Father, I want to complete the work you have for me. As I reflect on the privilege and the wonder of co-laboring with you for eternal good, my heart is moved with …*
> *Continue to reveal yourself to me as I impart your life and love to those I serve.*

L-4 Rejoicing regularly in my identity as His beloved

SPIRIT-
EMPOWERED
Faith

A PERSONAL CONFESSION

By the early 1990s, the only indicator of spiritual awakening not present in North America was number five, "When Christians confess their sins to one another." Yet that was about to change.

As the Crusade in Seattle was concluded in April 1991, and

my attention shifted to the Crusade in Portland, I began to hear about some unusual meetings in which pastors had come together and openly confessed practically every sin known to man.

It was eye-opening, and to be honest, it put me on guard. So many times I had seen confession lead to gossip. Yet, as I learned about these extraordinary times of confession, gossip was nowhere to be heard. There could be only one explanation. When the white-hot light of God's Spirit of conviction fell on His people, when one person confessed his sin, all were convicted to whatever degree they were guilty. The result was that no one was excluded from conviction or confession, and cleansing came to everyone.

The man behind these Pastors' Prayer Summits was Dr. Joe Aldrich, president of Multnomah Bible College in Salem, Oregon. I met Joe in a small, leadership team meeting to discuss how we might pray for an upcoming Crusade in Portland. Within minutes "Dr. Joe," as he was commonly known, presented us with a remarkable vision of how concerted, organized prayer could unify a city and build the greatest Crusade possible.

That morning, Dr. Joe revealed the answer in these words as he read aloud: "How good and how pleasant *it is* for brethren to dwell together in unity!" (Psalm 133:1). Then he asked the group, "Guys, what would it take for a bunch of us to get together?" Almost immediately, the pastors responded with a question of their own, "That's what we want. How do we do it?"

"I had been involved in pastors' conferences before," says Joe. "Often the participants would leave feeling tremendously blessed. They'd fly back home to their city, alone, without coming together with their fellow pastors where they lived."[2]

Several months after the Salem meeting, Joe added the practical exclamation mark to the pastors' response by inviting them and other ministers from the area to a conference center for a weekend retreat. The participants were "'one in Spirit' in the deepest sense I'd ever seen because we spent time with the Lord. It finally dawned on me to get these Salem-area pastors involved in the holiness of God, whatever it took."[3]

As a result, Joe made sure there was no keynote speaker. He planned no special music. "In fact," he recalls, "there was not a single musical instrument! That weekend, we were willing to gamble and let the Spirit of God be the Spirit of God in our midst." That first Pastors' Prayer Summit could not have been scripted in advance because the events that unfolded over the next two days were totally unrehearsed and totally of God. In a very awesome way, truth was stranger than fiction.

There was lots of time for singing, lots of time for prayer, lots of time for God to speak to ministers who were living a bad dream and who needed to be awakened.

"In one service," Aldrich recalls, "a pastor came to me during communion, grabbed my knee and said, 'Joe, there are seven churches that my church has grievously sinned against. I need to ask forgiveness of each of those pastors, personally.' After collecting himself, this pastor stood up before the gathering and said, 'My church has spoken against some of you and your ministries. That is wrong. We have sinned. Will you forgive me?'"

"Not only was there forgiveness, but this one pastor's words touched off reciprocal confessions."

Adrich goes on to share another story. "Another time, we were just ready to start communion when a charismatic pastor stood up and said, 'I don't think any of us should take communion tonight. We know we've spoken against each other; we've undercut each other, and we, of all people, should know that we are not to partake in an unworthy manner.' After that, pastor after pastor asked forgiveness of each other. I saw one charismatic pastor lying on the carpet, face down, crying to the Lord, 'I'm empty, I'm barren, I need to be filled and restored.'"

"Confession before God is a great leveler among Christians," admits Joe. "Non-charismatic pastors had to admit, 'This charismatic knows his Bible. He loves The Book. He loves the same songs I do. He's my brother!' On this extraordinary weekend the stereotypes, the prejudices that kept these fellow-Christian leaders apart for years, began to disappear."[4]

The word spread and several other prayer summits were held within the next few months. Terry Dirks directed International Renewal Ministries, which would eventually lead to Pastors' Prayer Summits throughout the country. Observing the first few meetings, Dirks said, "We began to see that God had placed in the hearts of His people a hunger for Himself. Men said, 'It's not business as usual. We don't need more seminars and conferences. We need a fresh touch of God in heaven-sent revival.' "

Through the Prayer Summits, Joe Aldrich, Terry Dirks, and many others discovered a critical relationship between the initial stirrings of a fresh, spiritual awakening in America and full-blown revival. If past revivals in our country are any indication of what's to come, the brokenness and restoration ministers are finding through the Pastors' Prayer Summits will lead to evangelism that brings others into a personal relationship with God through Jesus Christ.

As Joe Aldrich summarized so well, "In this movement we're watching, there is a desire to see God really impact a community. But to impact a community, we must *be* a community. To be a community, we must have unity. To have unity, we must have humility. And to have humility, we must rediscover holiness."[5]

Community based on unity, unity built on humility, humility rooted in holiness!

This progression of faith summarizes so well the way God is breathing new life into our nation's pastoral leaders—by bringing them to their knees. The words of one Prayer Summit participant suggest why these remarkable gatherings are synonymous with true, spiritual awakening: "We came to pray," he wrote, "but we beheld Jesus. I arrived as a pastor. I departed as a believer. No amount of words could explain the depth, the warmth, the love, the mutual care that has been imparted as we have looked to the Lord of the church."

WHOA, CANADA!

In 1986, George Derksen was a thirty-five-year-old publisher from Toronto, Ontario, Canada. For years, he had produced attractive magazines. Because he wanted to put his talents into something that people wouldn't throw away, he developed an idea to produce a book unlike anything he had ever done. He designed *The Why Book* as an attractive, 150-page "coffee table book" to lead readers to ask the central question, "Why am I on this earth?" It was his way of reaching out with the gospel. At Expo '86, the World's Fair in Vancouver, British Columbia, 10,000 copies of *The Why Book* were distributed at the Pavilion of Promise. Another 130,000 copies were distributed throughout Winnipeg, Manitoba.

Two years later, a tele poll revealed startling findings:

- When asked if *The Why Book* was still in their home, 65 percent of the people said, "Yes."
- Sixteen percent said they had signed a commitment card (attached in the back of the book), to receive Jesus Christ as their personal Lord and Savior.
- The most remarkable discovery, however, was this: When those signing the commitment cards were asked if they had learned of anyone who had been praying for them, according to George, a majority said, "Yes, someone was praying."[6]

"My prayer is that God will revive the people of Canada and save our country," says George. "My prayer is that Canada will be known as a country of prayer."[7]

JIM THARP'S SCHOOL OF PRAYER

In 1975, I met Jim Tharp, a senior pastor at a church in Albuquerque, New Mexico. Throughout the years, our friendship deepened. In 1986, our paths crossed again as I was in the midst of directing the "Peaks to Plains" Billy Graham Crusade, a five-state evangelistic outreach to Montana, North Dakota, South Dakota, Colorado, and Wyoming. Right away, I could tell there was something unusual about Jim. He told me he had recently met with some fellow pastors in a "pastoral institute," sponsored by his denomination. The focus of the conference had been prayer. One Christian man had completed forty days of prayer and fasting and told the group about it. Jim said the man's testimony and the prayer he experienced over those days had gripped him. "Never before had I majored in prayer," he said, "but I began to discover something of the power of prayer as seen in the life of our Lord and the early church."[8]

Jim couldn't contain his excitement. He created an eight-hour seminar called a "School of Prayer." In the school, Jim distinguished Great Awakenings (which he defines as "mighty movings of the Holy Spirit who falls on sinners in the land") from revivals ("the spiritual renewal of the church itself"). He also described spiritual warfare and how a Christian could establish a discipline of prayer and Bible study. The School of Prayer seminars became so popular throughout the US Jim resigned his pastorate to invest more time in teaching on prayer. He taught and encouraged thousands to pray.[9]

NELL BARR: POWER PLANT

"For years I viewed prayer as just another part of being a Christian, like reading the Bible at dinner. The School of Prayer revolutionized our prayer life," says Nell Barr, who developed the discipline of praying one hour each morning with her husband. "At the end of the hour I don't leave the prayer time; Jesus just continues to walk with me."[10]

Nell remembers when Jim told the story of the renowned pastor Charles Spurgeon who, while giving people a tour of his church prior to his sermons, led them down into the basement. "Here, I want you to see the power plant of the church," he said. When Spurgeon opened the door, there was a roomful of men and women deep in prayer. After hearing the story, Nell Barr felt moved by the Holy Spirit to form a similar "power plant" of continuous pray-ers who would intercede during all eight hours of Tharp's annual School of Prayer session in Bozeman, Montana. As she said, "Every time we step into that prayer room, we step out of a realm of time and into a realm of communion."[11]

Walking
in the Light
of God's
Son

For as many as are the promises of God, in Him [Jesus] they are yes.
(2 Corinthians 1:20 NASB)

Pause and ask God to reveal Jesus to you from His Word. Ask Him to show you how He is One who is humble and gentle (Matthew 11:28–29).

God, I want to see and encounter Jesus in your Word. I know your Word is living and active (Hebrews 4:14). Do a work in me so that I have your humility, your gentleness and your holiness, so that I might join you in this Jesus-Now Awakening. Thank you for hearing and for answering (John 15:7).

W-6 Fresh, frequent, transforming encounters with the Christ of Scripture

MAC PIER: PRAYER FOR THE CITY

Before Mac Pier became the president of New York City Leadership Center, he headed the Concerts of Prayer for Greater New York. Mac has steeped himself in the urban setting and his boots-on-the-ground appreciation of God on the move cannot be missed.

The church in the urban arena is really reflecting the major global trends of the growth of Christendom, particularly in the eastern and southern hemispheres. In New York City, for example, there are two thousand five hundred Hispanic congregations and large numbers of Korean churches, not to mention thousands of African American churches. The percentage of non-white, active, orthodox Protestants is probably 92 percent, so the demographics of the church in urban US really mirror what's happening globally.[12]

The church Mac attends in Flushing, for example, is very diverse. He shares, "We have five congregations and people speak as many as sixteen languages in one congregation. So we have some examples of that, particularly in parts of the city where there is a lot of diversity. Queens and certain parts of the Bronx are very diverse. The upshot is that *integration*, not discrimination, is the watchword for today's imminent spiritual awakening.

"For the most part," says Pier, "most churches in New York are still what we call 'tribal' in that Africans worship with Africans, Chinese worship with Chinese. There are some exceptions to that. So on a week-to-week basis, most people tend to worship with people who look like themselves. But there are significant expressions of churches doing outside things together, whether it's an event, or a project, coming together for conferences. So there is a lot of cross-pollination happening together at that level."[13]

Stitched into the weave of this multi-ethnic faith network is prayer. "We started with our first Concert of Prayer in February of 1988, and since then well over 200,000 people who attended various expressions of the Concerts of Prayer movement," says Pier. "We started by inviting sixteen churches to come together and pray, and seventy-five churches showed up. Within two years, churches in each of New York's five boroughs, plus Long Island and New Jersey were gathering regularly to pray."[14]

Pier and countless other Jesus-followers in Gotham know that God's faithfulness to touch and transform New York City through the prayers of His faithful children is nothing new. "In 1995, we started a daily prayer vigil patterned after the Moravian Movement and Isaiah 62:6–7:

I have set watchmen on your walls, O Jerusalem;
They shall never hold their peace day or night.
You who make mention of the Lord, do not keep silent,
And give Him no rest till He establishes
And till He makes Jerusalem a praise in the earth.

In 1727, twenty-four Moravians began a twenty-four-hour prayer vigil that lasted one hundred years. We began a daily prayer, involving one hundred churches. Today, here in 2014, it's still going strong. During the first five years of the prayer vigil, we saw the murder rate in New York City drop by 70 percent. Up until 1994, we had been the most violent city in America, with about 2,400 murders annually. Six years later, we were considered the safest city in America of more than a million people. We attribute this to what was happening spiritually."[15]

Fervent, faithful, uninterrupted prayer has meant something more. "There's a parallel relationship between the prayer movement and the church planting movement. We've had about ten denominations working together, and throughout New York City we've helped incubate about one hundred new churches in the last three years alone. This is significant (even though the greater New York City region is 21.5 million people), so we recognize the need to do more."[16]

How far and wide has this prayer-fed spiritual fire begun to spread? John Robb with the International Council of Prayer offers a 30,000-foot view, explaining that the Global Day of Prayer brought half a billion people together in prayer. Dale Schlafer, president of World Revival and Awakening, adds a needed exclamation point: "If it's God who sets His people to pray, it must mean God is going to answer these prayers. He wouldn't waste time on something He doesn't intend to answer. Sometimes we get discouraged. What keeps me in the game is believing maybe this prayer is the one that tips it!"

DAVID BRYANT'S CONCERTS OF PRAYER

In 1988, David Bryant left InterVarsity Christian Fellowship to devote his complete time and effort to nurturing what he sensed was a grassroots prayer movement. He founded Concerts of Prayer International (COPI) "to serve the church by promoting, equipping and mobilizing movements of united prayer that seek God for spiritual awakening and worldwide evangelization."[17]

Bryant himself writes, "Historically speaking, the primary focus of Concerts has been on two major agendas: Christians prayed for Christ's *fullness* (Ephesians 1:22–23) to be revealed in His church to empower them to accomplish the task that was before them. They also prayed for the *fulfillment* (Ephesians 1:10) of His saving purposes among the nations through an awakened, consecrated church. The same twofold agenda prevails today.

"And so Concerts of Prayer helps describe Christians united on a regular basis to seek fullness and fulfillment. Extraordinary, united prayer is not determined so much by how long one prays or how often, but rather that Christians do pray, that they pray for those things most on God's heart, and that they do so together—'in concert.'"[18]

Practically speaking, Concerts of Prayer took the form of large, public meetings, usually in a church building. Typically, each concert followed a structured, two-hour format:

- Celebration (ten minutes)
- Preparation (twenty minutes)
- Dedication (five minutes)
- Seeking for Fullness/Awakening in the church (thirty minutes)
- Seeking for Fulfillment/Mission among the Nations (thirty minutes)
- Testimonies: What has God said to us here? (ten minutes)
- Grand Finale (fifteen minutes)

Concerts of Prayer have played an important part of the current, ongoing prayer movement in America. Through the vision and efforts of David Bryant and the ministry he's founded, many

Christians, who perhaps wouldn't otherwise, have come together in prayer.

A FEAST OF PRAYER AND FASTING

"I am convinced that God will soon send a great spiritual awakening to our country and the world ... ."[19]

These words came from Bill Bright, founder and director of Campus Crusade for Christ International. In a warm yet urgent three-page letter, Bill had invited Christian leaders in the United States to join him from December 5–7, 1994, for three days of prayer and fasting in Orlando, Florida.

The names of seventy-two distinguished Christian men and women who made up the Invitation Committee told me that this gathering would be a first in recent memory. But it was Bill's own story that convinced me I had to attend:

> For me, the call to fast and pray for our nation began in earnest on July 5, 1994, when I began a forty-day fast for revival and awakening in America and the fulfillment of the Great Commission throughout the world. On the morning that I began my twenty-ninth day of fasting I was reading in 2 Chronicles, chapters 28–30, when God's holy Word spoke to my heart in a most unusual way.
>
> Like ancient Judah, our nation is rapidly becoming morally and spiritually destitute. As I read that Hezekiah, King of Judah, wrote a letter to the leaders of Israel and Judah inviting them to join him in celebrating the Passover in the newly opened, cleansed and dedicated temple—which his evil father, Ahaz, had closed—I felt impressed by the Lord to write letters to hundreds of the most influential Christians in this country, inviting them

to gather in Orlando, as guests of Campus Crusade, to fast and pray. We do not have a political agenda.

This will be strictly a time for fasting and prayer and for seeking God's direction on how we, His servants, can be instruments of revival for our nation and the world. By God's grace, this could be one of the most significant prayer and fasting gatherings in modern history.[20]

I accepted Bill's invitation and went to Florida. Based on all that happened in Orlando, I can say that, by God's grace, Bill's hope and prayer came true. As one of nearly seven hundred participants, I witnessed an unusual display of Christian leaders across the denominational and parachurch spectrum. That unity was expressed best by author/speaker Kay Arthur who gave the memorable illustration of two different heart tissues beating at different rhythms, yet when they physically touch each other, they beat in unison. "When we touch Jesus," she says, "we pump the same."

Today, more and more of these people are saying, "There is such a desperation in our world, it's time we got on our faces with one another to break down barriers and build bonds of love and trust."[21]

The biblical evidence of Hezekiah and others *shows that revival is of God.*

The historical precedence of former Great Awakenings *suggests that revival in our nation could come again.*

The reality that our ever-darkening world is now being pierced by extraordinary truth *indicates that the early light of revival is already dawning.*

I can hear at least three distinctive voices of prayer, three unmistakable expressions of the Holy Spirit beckoning and bringing the young and the old—all ages and stages in between—to Jesus. As you read their stories, notice what unites Nick Hall, a college student-turned evangelist; Karen Cover, a faithful, persevering pray-er in Hollywood; Bill Eubank, a lay pastor, and Bruce Snell a businessman.

"JESUS, WILL YOU RESET MY LIFE?"

When Nick Hall was a junior at North Dakota State University, he wrote a paper in an English class about envisioning a student-led, campus-wide initiative to present the gospel of Jesus to classmates. Eight thousand people filled the Bison Sports Arena, and 1,200 students gave their lives to Christ.

PULSE, an evangelism ministry founded on prayer, was born. PULSE exists to awaken culture to the reality of Jesus. By 2015, the movement had grown to impact more than thirty university campuses and more than 250,000 people. Where is prayer? It is at the center, as the group's newsletter makes clear: "At every PULSE event, we refer to our prayer room as 'The Engine Room' because we believe this is where our power comes from. This room is typically unseen by most attendees, located in a classroom or closet at the venue. Regardless of its location, 'The Engine Room' is always filled with faithful intercessors, asking for God's blessing toward the harvest.

Chris McFarland, Executive Vice President of PULSE, notes, "Jesus said, 'My house shall be called a house of prayer,' and His disciples witnessed firsthand the power of Jesus' prayer life as they asked Him, 'Lord, would you teach us to pray?' For anyone wanting to follow Jesus, prayer must take priority."[22]

PULSE is the ministry behind the RESET Movement and the Together 2016 gathering at the National Mall in Washington, DC on July 16, 2016. It was a day of unified prayer and worship rallying a generation around Jesus and a call for a supernatural reset in lives, culture, and our nation.

Rather than resorting to the "we" of an organization, the RESET message focuses on the "you" each and every individual who is invited to pray the RESET Prayer: "Jesus, will you reset my life? My thoughts? My priorities? My school? My fears?" With its focus on making new, individual relationships with Jesus, RESET has introduced a fresh, new language of personal revival. (For more information, visit pulsemovement.com.)

KAREN COVELL: IN A LEADING ROLE

Whether it's a career, a budding romance or life's final chapter, most people would gladly love a Hollywood ending. Fade in to Karen Covell whose genesis in ministry called for a surprise Hollywood *beginning*. She set out wanting to produce live theater before plying her craft in television and film. Then, fourteen years ago she felt some new inner stirrings. Prayer, which had always been such a part of her Christian life, became a driving passion.

I began to ask others to pray with me for those working in Hollywood—producers, directors, actors, writers, and technicians. I got a lot of pushback from believers outside of Hollywood. Many Christians I met wanted nothing to do with the entertainment industry, mainly because of the kind of movies they didn't like coming out of Hollywood. They weren't shy, either, telling me, "You're wasting your time praying for celebrities."[23]

Covell persisted. Down, though not defeated, she prayed that God would massage and soften the hearts of Christian believers who had backed away and declined to pray. In 2001, she founded the Hollywood Prayer Network. Over time, online connections sprang up, churches inquired, trusted relationships grew, and prayer groups formed. Today, the Network's ministry has more than 20,000 praying members, and they have matched 1,800 one-to-one prayer partnerships—individuals, each of whom prays regularly for a person in the entertainment industry. There's a reason, Covell believes, why prayer avoidance has given way to prayer involvement.

BILL EUBANK: THE GIFT OF INTERCESSION

Bill Eubank was driving in the car near his home of Charlotte, North Carolina, when he realized he wasn't alone.

> I heard the Lord say, "You need to be involved in a group of men to pray for greater Charlotte region." I began to listen to what was going on, both inside me and in our area. I joined a group of four men, two of which were pastors, to intercede for our city. Thirty years later, we're still praying. In the past five or six years, we've sensed very strongly that God wants to move again through our region of the country. There's a sense that God wants to pull out all the stops, invade society, and touch those who know Him.[24]

Might Bill's own words be the encouragement you and others need to turn to God and trust God in and through intercessory prayer?

> If you are born again, you are God's son or daughter (John 1:12). As His child, you have a direct "hotline" to God. At any time, you can boldly come into His presence (Hebrews 4:16). This incredible access to God is the basis for intercession. Once you are in God's presence, you can now discover His battle plan for the situation you are facing. Because prayer alone is not enough—you need a target for your prayers!
> To discover God's plan, all you have to do is ask. The Bible says "If any of you need wisdom, you should ask

God, and it will be given to you" (James 1:5). When we ask God for wisdom, His desires will become the focus of our prayers. "Let God change the way you think. Then you will know how to do everything that is good and pleasing to Him" (Romans 12:2).

Intercession involves taking hold of God's will and refusing to let go until His will comes to pass. Intercessory prayer is not the same as prayers for yourself, or for 'enlightenment,' or for spiritual gifts, or for guidance, or any personal matter, or any glittering generality.

Intercession is not just praying for someone else's needs. Intercession is praying with the real hope and real intent that God would step in and act for the positive advancement of some specific other person or groups of people or community. It is trusting God to act, even if it's not in the manner or timing we seek. God wants us to ask, even urgently. It is casting our weakness before God's strength, and (at its best) having a bit of God's passion burn in us.[25]

On page 200–202, you'll find some practical resources to pray, including helpful tips from Bill Eubank. Included are suggestions for establishing "Prayer Etiquette" for corporate and intercessory prayer. The second list includes some insights and lessons Bill and others have learned over the past thirty years of weekly intercessory prayer.

NEW MORNING OF REVIVAL

Bruce Snell is a businessman who loves getting rousted out of bed at 3:00 a.m. "I have this intimacy with Jesus. Seven days a week, He awakens me in the dark. An uninterrupted time of prayer follows. I talk to Him. I tell Him the things that are on my heart about my family, my work, my life, but most of all, I ask Jesus, 'What is it that you are speaking to me, Lord. What is it ... that you ... are speaking ... to me?'"

"One morning, the Lord Jesus said to me, 'The altar, Bruce, stay at the altar.'"

"At the altar is where we are altered! At the altar of prayer is where I leave everything that weighs on me. At the altar is where I reach out and reach up and bring everything, every praise, every concern, every longing, every sorrow, every joy to Jesus. I leave it all with Him, and I leave it all in prayer."[26]

Do you see more clearly why prayer is the heartbeat of both personal revival and the Great Awakening now before us?

Charles Finney noted that revival is simply normal Christianity. In a normal family relationship, you expect clear communication between all the members. For the Christian, prayer is that clear line of communication in an intimate relationship with God. We see in the parable of the Prodigal Son specifically how prayer shows the early beginnings of revival. As the son returned home and reestablished his communication and relationship with the father, the father turned to the elder son and said, "Your brother was dead and is alive again, and was lost and is found" (Luke 15:32). The Greek word for "alive again" is *anazaho*, which means "brought back to life." So, what the father really meant was that his son was now revived!

Perhaps without knowing it, these Christians are experiencing the fact that prayer is always the most telling gauge of spiritual awakening. Why does God want us, as individuals, to pray so that He can corporately address the needs of His prodigal church? It's beyond us. It's beyond human understanding why God would want our silent longings and muttered whispers. Yet, He does. And through our prayer, revival begins.

Prayer unleashes power.

Power is necessary for the revitalization of the church.

A revitalized church is a unified and Christ-focused church.

A unified and Christ-focused church is necessary for evangelism.

Evangelism is necessary for discipleship.

Discipleship is necessary for a maturing, reproducing church.

A maturing, reproducing church is necessary for the building of the kingdom.

And the building of the kingdom is necessary for the return of Christ.

Revitalization, evangelism, discipleship, and building the kingdom for His return—it all begins in prayer—prayer that begins in the heart of God and moves to the heart of the Christian, whose heart is turned toward God. It begins in the heart of people like Nick Hall, Bill Eubank, Karen Covell, Mac Pier, and Bruce Snell. Each has invited others to pray in adoration, praise, confession, and repentance before our Lord. This is how personal revival begins and how a Great Awakening spreads.

"OH, GOD ..."

- Seven hundred Christian leaders gather to fast and pray together for three days in Orlando, Florida.
- A handful of tired pastors meet for breakfast in Salem, Oregon.
- Four men meet for prayer every Saturday morning for thirty years.
- A businessman is rousted from his bed at 3:00 a.m., only to get down on his knees and bring his entire self to the altar.

The stirring power of prayer in America today is defined by everyday people such as these.

It happened on the Hebrides Islands, off the western coast of Scotland in 1947. A group of five to seven very godly men had become concerned about their home and country. Sadly, they felt that the Spirit of God was absent. They were despondent about their friends' indifference to the gospel and their nation's indifference to spiritual things. These men realized that the needs were so far beyond them that their only hope, their only answer, was to go before God.

Sacrificially, these few common men began to pray. After working all day, they would go home for dinner and dedicate the evening to their families. Then, around ten o'clock, when they were tired and ready to go to bed, they would walk out into the night and meet together in a lighted barn. There they would pray—sometimes five, sometimes six, sometimes seven of them. For two long years, they went to the barn, night after night. In the heat of summer and in the briskness of fall, in the chill of winter and in the cool of spring, these sacrificing, godly men met together on their knees.

"Oh, God," they cried out, "do something for our islands."

Every time they prayed they always read a passage of Scripture, and they prayed until they had peace in their hearts. One night in 1949, two years after they had begun meeting, as they gathered in the barn, one of the men opened his Bible to Psalm 24 and began to read. "The earth is the LORD's, and the fullness thereof; the world, and they that dwell therein. For he hath founded it upon the seas, and established it upon the floods. Who shall ascend into the hill of the LORD? Or who shall stand in his holy place? He that hath clean hands, and a pure heart; who hath not lifted up his soul unto vanity, nor sworn deceitfully" (Psalm 24:1–4).

Suddenly the truth hit these men. "Is it possible," they asked, "that for two long years we've been praying night after night, sacrificially, for the Lord to move on our islands—and yet our hands are not clean? Is it possible our hearts are not pure? Is it possible that our souls have been lifted up to vanity and that we have sworn deceitfully?" That moment, the Lord convicted them that all the things they feared were true. That night, they prayed the words from the book of James, "Therefore confess your sins to one other and pray for one another that you may be healed. The prayer of a righteous person has great power as it is working" (5:16 ESV).

History records that these men left the barn that night, and on the way to the village, they topped the hill and looked down the road. There, in the ditch, they saw two town drunks on their knees, stumbling and mumbling. As the believers came closer, they realized the two men weren't drunk at all. They were sober, and they were praying. They were on their knees, under conviction of sin, asking God to forgive them.

"The prayer of a righteous man is powerful and effective!"

The men, who had prayed every night for months, looked out over the night sky and saw the homes below. At 1:30 a.m., lights in the village were on. The people had awakened from their sleep. Dozens of families, realizing their separation from God, had gotten up from their beds in consternation to try to find someone awake with whom they could talk. Night became dawn, and the next morning, people knew that something had changed. The people invited Duncan Campbell, the great evangelist from England, to visit their homeland. He came, preached, and great revival broke out—a revival that was born through prayer in a barn.[27]

Might the Holy Spirit already be at work in you drawing you to Himself, stirring you to pray, moving you to pray for a fresh awakening, a new touch of God?

What do you think God could do in your life, your church,

your nation, if you began praying for revival? No one knows the answer—yet. But one thing is absolutely certain:

- If the moral deterioration expressed through corruption, lying, violence, and greed in our nation grieves you,
- If the growing indifference to the good news of salvation saddens you,
- If the break-up of marriages, families, and other cherished relationships hurts you,
- If these and other sorrows have stirred in you a new hunger for God,

You are not alone.

If your prayer is that our nation turns from its prodigal ways and comes home to a loving Father, if your heart beats in unison with the people about whom you've been reading, then you are part of the Pastors' Prayer Summits. You are part of Nell Barr's early morning-prayer time. You are part of anyone and everyone who meets before work to pray for their country, their city, and their church.

You are already part of this Jesus-Now Awakening!

Be filled with expectation and hope for all that God is now unfolding in North America and all that is yet to come. Be glad, and *be aware*. The current spiritual awakening is not without potential obstacles and threats that can cause spiritual blindness. Imagine Jesus standing before you, close enough to reach out and touch. You simply walk past Him because something has seriously harmed your vision, which means you don't have eyes to see. Because He has loved you since forever, He turns around and calls your name. But because something has damaged your hearing, you keep walking, unaware that it's Jesus calling you, calling you to turn around, calling you to Him.

How would you feel? What would you do if you had eyes to see and ears to hear?

Isn't it time we looked at what on earth could be keeping you and me from joining Jesus in the great Jesus-Now Awakening that's already begun?

Yet the LORD longs to be gracious to you;
therefore he will rise up to show you compassion.
For the LORD is a God of justice.
Blessed are all who wait for him! (Isaiah 30:18 NIV)

Consider the current challenges and struggles in your world and in your life. Are you losing hope in relationships, religion, or politics? Are you struggling at work, with your family, in your accomplishments, or your faith? Whatever your challenge, meditate on the Lord of hosts, who longs to show you grace and rises to show you compassion. Invite Christ into your struggle. Together, with other followers of Jesus, make a personal request for Jesus to show Himself to you in the midst of those challenges.

In the quietness of this time, close your eyes and imagine the picture of the resurrected Christ. He is excited to express His personal grace and divine favor just for you. Imagine the scene of Jesus rising to receive you with welcoming arms! Pause to picture this moment between you and Jesus. Notice the tenderness of His expression and that Christ longs to give you grace. Hear the gentleness in His voice as He confirms His great compassion for you. Now, with a partner or small group, give Jesus thanks for such an incredible blessing just for you! Tell Him about your gratefulness.

Jesus, as I imagine you standing up to receive me with welcoming arms, I am grateful because ...

*I am thankful when I see the tenderness in your face and hear
the compassion in your voice because … I am moved with gratitude for how you …*

**L-3 Experiencing God as He really is
through deepened intimacy with Him**

SIX

Potential Obstacles Ahead

f I had to name someone who had his finger on the pulse of revival stirrings in North America in recent years, it would be Dr. Lewis Drummond. This respected, godly scholar wrote several noted books on revival and has held the Billy Graham Chair of Evangelism and Church Growth at Beeson Divinity School (Samford University) in Birmingham, Alabama since 1991. I met Dr. Drummond in Louisville, Kentucky, in 1976. As a member of the faculty of Southern Baptist Theological Seminary, he held the original Billy Graham Chair of Evangelism.

At the time, talk of spiritual awakening in this country was almost non-existent. "There was not near as much interest in revival or prayer back then as there is today," he said in 1994.[1] Even then, Dr. Drummond was already seeing the kind of revival stirrings that preceded our nation's Great Awakenings. In the popular press, a *Newsweek* magazine cover proclaimed, "The Search for the Sacred: America's Quest for Spiritual Meaning."[2]

Says Drummond,

> I'm seeing at least two things I've never seen in my lifetime, two things that make me think America may

be ripe for a new spiritual awakening. First, there's never been so much concern and interest in revival. I'm seeing this renewed interest in pastors, and to some extent, in laypersons as well.

The second thing that's remarkable about the potential for revival in America is the increasing interest in prayer and the formation of prayer groups throughout our nation. Though it's still in the developmental stage, there's so much prayer for revival today.[3]

And to think Drummond was speaking twenty-five years *before* prayer movements like RESET were set to blossom and spread. From this highly organized movement in the spotlight of the national media to the quietest church gathering about which you or I will never know, people are hoping for a new breath of God for their individual lives, their cities, and their nation.[4]

When it comes to revival, many of today's Jesus-followers are asking, "Where will it all lead? How close is our country to a full-blown, Jesus-Now Awakening?"

This genuine enthusiasm is a double-edged sword. In the coming days, all of the interest, desire, and prayers for God to revive our land could become nothing more than the spiritual equivalent of "one step forward, two steps back" if we don't see the very real, unseen obstacles to revival that are in our midst. Whether America's next Great Awakening is coming next year or in the next century, every Christian who prays for revival will face obstacles sooner or later. The potential barriers are so deceptively present that I believe they could be keeping you and I from seeing, from even experiencing, what God is doing in our nation *right now*. As we explore five obstacles to a Jesus-Now Awakening, let's anticipate them, so that we can overcome them.

OBSTACLE 1
"WE CAN DO THIS THING!"

The obstacles I'm painfully aware of lurk in the enthusiasm of well-intentioned Christians who genuinely want more of God. Lewis Drummond articulated what has happened in the church today.

"At one stage in my ministry, I preached on 2 Chronicles 7:14, 'If my people, who are called by My name, will humble themselves and pray and seek My face and turn from their wicked ways, then will I hear from heaven, and will forgive their sin and will heal their land.' I stressed that if you do these things—humble, pray, seek God's face, and turn from your wicked ways—you will have revival. In actuality, these things are not the prerequisites to revival; they *are* the revival; the forgiving of sins and the healing of land *are the results*.

> But here's what I think has happened. Though individually we are to humble ourselves, pray, seek God's face and turn from our wicked ways, many Christians, particularly pastors, have fallen into what author, preacher, and theologian Stephen Olford calls "evangelical humanism." This is a determined, well-meaning faith that says, "We can do this thing! We can grow our church! We can be the people God wants us to be." Such an "if/then" approach says, "If you do these five things, God's blessing is bound to happen." While humility, prayer, seeking after God, and repenting from our wickedness are things God calls us to do, merely trying to 'work them out the best we can' may stand in the way of real revival.[5]

Drummond recalled how, in the early 1960s, the Spirit was cut short in a free church in England. "During worship on this particular Sunday, I saw people being convicted of their own brokenness and sin. They really began to weep. The pastor may have been unfamiliar with the work of the Spirit, or he may have just been plain scared to death because he put a stop to the people's expressiveness. He chastised these confessing Christians for their tears and, in so doing, curtailed the awakening work of the Spirit in the congregation."[6]

A second instance of revival cut short took place closer to home. Drummond remembered when revival began to break out at a theological seminary in the United States. Unrelated to the Spirit's movement on campus, one student who was either demonic or psychotic said to his peers, "I'm going to get on the roof of the men's dormitory, and I'll jump off and float down to the ground and bring a great revival."

"It was the identical temptation of Jesus on the pinnacle of the temple," said Drummond. Except this young man didn't float, he fell hard to the ground and broke his leg. The incident alarmed the administration. Instead of realizing this was a satanic attack, they stopped all prayer groups for revival.[7]

The relevant questions we need to be asking ourselves are these:

- Do I long for God's forgiveness and healing in this country—a movement that can come only from Him?
- Do I want to be part of an extraordinary movement of the Holy Spirit in this nation?

If your answer to both is yes, if deeper spiritual life is what you seek, then be ready to experience two very distinct and opposing forces in this Jesus-Now Awakening. God's infinite desire to bring our nation to Himself and our imperfect human nature that causes us to look out for ourselves.

Walking
in the Light
of God's
Son

Without Me you can do nothing. (John 15:5)

Consider again, this obstacle for renewal: "We believe that we can do this thing."

Pause quietly to imagine these words from Jesus. Imagine the Savior speaking directly to you about how you might be a part of the Jesus-Now Awakening. What evidences of self-effort or pride might Jesus see in you? What does He want you to see, hear, or experience instead? Meditate on His words: "Without Me you can do nothing."

Ask Jesus to change, strengthen, and empower you.

Now celebrate as you hear Jesus whisper these words to your spirit: Remember, "with God all things are possible" (Matthew 19:26).

Receive the joy of this promise, and let it catalyze your hope for awakening. Wait to sense His presence and power in all of your life.

**L-10 Practicing the presence of the Lord,
yielding to the Spirit's work of Christ-likeness**

OBSTACLE 2
REASON HAS ITS LIMITS

The second potential obstacle to personal and national spiritual revival is as basic as our desire to know God. It is the need to understand.

North Americans are influenced strongly by the Greek, rationalistic tradition that essentially says, the most effective way of knowing something or someone is through the mind. The mind is the avenue of knowledge, the mechanism on which we depend to know ourselves, others, our world, and our God. This rationalistic heritage is so embedded in who we are that we often make our analytical thinking processes synonymous with belief. Thus our faith tends to follow a logical, rational path. If we want to know who God is and what He is about, we tend to process our understanding something like this:

- Observe—become aware of all that's in and around us
- Take in—receive all the data we can gather
- Organize—arrange the assorted thoughts, feelings, and questions
- Analyze—look closely to sort out what we want to accept or reject
- Understand—conclude what's real, what's true, what we can use

Rick Marshall is not a person to rely on experience alone. At the Cannon Beach Christian Conference Center in Cannon Beach, Oregon, where approximately ten Philadelphia pastors joined 150 other ministers working on the Billy Graham Crusade in Portland, Rick's life was literally renewed. Rick knew God's Word extremely well. He had received training from the Navigators. Yet, at the conference, Rick, who had always approached things from a clear, rationalistic perspective, *experienced* the Holy Spirit. This gifted young leader, who had always come to the knowledge of faith and truth through reason, was supernaturally awakened to Jesus through conviction, confession, and repentance.

The convicting power of God that Rick experienced certainly did not negate his God-given ability to reason; it simply affirmed the principles of the Word he already knew and now fulfilled. One of those was "Be still, and know that I *am* God" (Psalm 46:10). Rick heard that "still small voice" (1 Kings 19:12) and confessed his sin, for which he received forgiveness. When God broke through, Rick realized that knowledge wasn't everything. What touched his heart, renewed his mind, and changed his life was a person-to-person experience with God, in Jesus Christ through the power of the Holy Spirit.

Simply put, our flawed, rationalistic minds cannot fully comprehend revival. Revival is not a mystery to be "thought through." It is a movement of the Spirit to be experienced with reverence, checked against the clear guidelines of Scripture, and then given to the God who alone deserves our praise. If we want to know this God, particularly in a season of awakening, we need to remember Jesus' words: "God *is* Spirit, and those who worship Him must worship in spirit and truth" (John 4:24).

How can we know the Spirit with organized, yet limited rationalistic minds? How can we use our minds to the fullest to understand revival, without limiting our understanding of God to what our minds can process? As you come to God through your own prayer, confession, and repentance, do not come to him with the Greek mindset that compartmentalizes life into body, soul, and spirit. Come to God with the mindset of the Hebrew, as a whole person made complete in God.

The Hebrew mindset did not compartmentalize body, mind, and soul. None of the three was any more or less important than the other two. All three comprised the one person. Our emotion, a vital part of one's soul to the Hebrew (distinct from emotionalism, which can be manufactured), would be as vital a part of your make-up as your mind. Rick Marshall could look at the Word of God and know what sin is. He could comprehend and identify sin. But only when Rick's personal emotions—the center of his being—were touched by the Holy Spirit, only when he saw himself as God saw him, only when he had disdain for the ungodly things in his life, could he be awakened. The same is true for you and me. A personal, Jesus-Now revival occurs when we allow God to have preeminence through the mind (knowledge), the body (obedience), and the soul (confession).

Walking
in the Light
of God's
Word

If anyone thinks that he knows anything, he knows nothing yet as he ought to know. (1 Corinthians 8:2)

Take a moment to remember a time when you were sure that you "knew" a Bible verse, only to discover that there was more to know! Share about this time with a partner or a small group.

I remember knowing that the Bible says ...

Only to discover that ...

For example: *I remember knowing that the Bible says that confessing my faults is good for relationships (James 5:16). Only to realize that it had been way too many months since I had actually experienced this verse. It had been too long since I had acknowledged any wrongs or regrets with my spouse.*

Just like the disciples, we often hear the Word and even receive it, but we stop short of the life-changing liberating power of experiencing it.

"I will delight in your decrees and not forget your word" (Psalm 119:16, NLT).

Disciples delight in walking in the light of God's Word, not forgetting how His truth has blessed them in areas of salvation, peace, and wisdom. Consider a specific Bible verse that has become especially meaningful to you. Then reflect on how God made it alive for you, leading you out of darkness into light.

- Perhaps God used a particular Bible verse (like John 3:16) to draw you out of sin's darkness into a new-birth encounter with Christ.
- Maybe God used a particular Bible promise (like Psalm 23) to lead you out of the valley of despair into more peaceful places of your life.
- Maybe God used a specific Bible admonition (like Ephesians 4:31) to challenge you to rid yourself of some area of darkness so that you could walk more closely with Him and hear His voice more often.

I'm grateful to God for using _____ (Scripture passage) in my life in order to lead me out of the darkness of _____ and into the light of _____.

After sharing your responses with a partner or small group, pray together. Express your gratitude for the power, promise, and potential of the light of God's Word.

W-7 A life explained as one of experiencing Scripture

OBSTACLE 3
STAND UP—OR REMAIN SEATED

A third potential obstacle to personal revival and spiritual awakening is the very real fear of not being accepted (and feeling rejected) by others.

In an age of conformity, the thought of speaking out and standing up for Jesus can be a truly ominous barrier. Imagine experiencing a new, deep sense of your own brokenness and your utter need for forgiveness and holiness. Imagine Jesus being so real, so close, and so alive that you begin to devour the Scriptures with a voracious desire to know Jesus in a way you've never known.

As you grow to know Him more, sins you once rationalized or ignored now feel like damaging, personal affronts to your best friend. You admit to Jesus your own desire to keep sinning even while you find a new willingness to turn your back on old patterns and walk in a new direction toward Jesus. This 180-degree turnaround is true repentance. When people want to know, "What's different with you?" you know the answer, and a thousand thoughts go through your mind, among them:

- What is he or she going to think about me once I start talking about God?
- I don't feel like I have the words to talk about Jesus even though I'm convinced what I believe by faith is of Jesus. What will I say?
- I'm afraid she's going to misunderstand.
- I'm afraid he won't accept me.
- What's going on inside because of the Lord is so undeniably real and so personal; I'm not sure I feel comfortable bringing it up.

This is the voice of wanting to be accepted. This is the deep human need to be liked by others. This is the willingness to be accepted even if it means silencing the undeniable truth that God is alive and at work in you.

I know this voice, this need, this willingness to be accepted all too well. Ever since I was a young seminary student, I've never had much of a problem opening my mouth to talk about God—except when it involved possible rejection. In twenty-plus years of ministry centered largely in evangelism, I've had literally thousands of opportunities to proclaim the wonderful salvation message of Jesus Christ to others. Yet, even though I know I'm telling the truth, and even though I know I'm helping someone go from darkness to light and from hell to heaven, I admit to myself I don't want to be rejected. My personal need for acceptance overrides my love for the person and the place of their eternal soul.

Though I am chagrined to admit this, I also know that I'm not alone. In fact, the reality of revival in our time raises this anxiety of personal rejection to new levels.

During the summer of 1992 in Buenos Aires, Argentina, I was one of more than a thousand believers packed inside a Baptist church for a pre-Billy Graham Crusade meeting. That evening, as a Presbyterian minister preached, God's Spirit began to move mightily in ways I had never observed. One moment, people were standing in the aisles lifting their hands in praise to God. The next moment, they were dropping to the floor, catatonic, without anyone touching them.

I saw it happen all around the room. There was no rhyme or reason why men and women were falling to the floor except that they were feeling a powerful touch of the Holy Spirit. I should have been celebrating this great work of God! Instead, I became terribly anxious inside. I looked around at people on either side of me who had fallen to the floor and were still seemingly unconscious and thought to myself, "Oh God, please don't touch me like *that*." Instead of praising God, I worried, "Oh God, don't let this happen to me. I don't want to be embarrassed!"

The reawakening that is to come and that may already be here won't hinge on whether today's image-conscious Christians go public with their convictions. God doesn't need to do an end-run around people's anxiety to be heard. I wonder how many of the one million teenage students who met for public prayer at their schools' flagpoles felt self-conscious by what their non-praying friends thought. For God, our lack of courage is not an ultimate obstacle to revival, but an opportunity to work through fragile egos and sweaty palms. So whether it's in a church in Argentina or in your own congregation, we can know that our need for human affirmation and acceptance is no obstacle for a God who is not ashamed to be seen with us. Even though He knows we are flawed vessels, He is ready to pour His Spirit into those who are willing to acknowledge the potter and be remade by Him.

OBSTACLE 4
WHO CARES ABOUT APATHY?

A fourth potential obstacle to personal and national spiritual awakening is apathy.

This disease of disinterest has been a nagging, disruptive gadfly to every revival in our nation's history. Apathy can take one of two forms: either a gradual familiarity with the extraordinary movement of the Holy Spirit or an overt disinterest in undeniable and extraordinary works of God. The first kind takes the form of a subtle comfort that breeds spiritual boredom and fatigue. The second kind is an overt disregard in caring about the obvious.

The first kind of apathy, a kind of spiritual descent of the heart, is one of the chief reasons that, without exception, nearly all revivals in history have never lasted more than a generation. Think of watching a spectacular Fourth of July fireworks display. We are awed by the first colorful explosions, entertained by the new few bursts, but bored by the time it's over. Though the explosions grow more spectacular and more elaborate, our interest wanes. At first, we think this is the greatest thing we've ever witnessed. After a while, when we've seen enough, we just want to get back to the car and beat the traffic home.

The second form of apathy is the overt variety that works

against revival before spiritual awakening has had a chance to emerge. This is the kind of apathy you hear today:

- *Revival? Taking place today? Never heard about it.*
- *Revival? Isn't that what they do at tent meetings with wild, screaming preachers?*
- *Revival seems like something out of history. What good have revivals ever done?*
- *Revival? Isn't that what evangelistic meetings held twice a year in the South are called?*

This kind of apathy erodes people's openness and anticipation for what God is already beginning to do in our land. More than indifference, apathy has the potential to blossom into true lack of concern, jealousy, and even antagonism. It's not a big stretch of the imagination to hear these voices speak out against even the mere possibility of a new, uncontained spiritual awakening.

Look at Joseph in the Old Testament. Were his brothers peeved that his dad gave him the coat of many colors because he was his daddy's favorite son? Yes! But what really made the brothers jealous was Joseph's description of his dreams, given to him by God, in which they bowed to him. They had been the ones who worked hard, who led their families, who sacrificed by spending nights out in the cold watching the sheep. Then to be told by a kid wearing a multicolored coat, "You're going to bow to me someday!"

When God inspires the "Josephs" of our day to personify the new, unfolding work of the Spirit, there will be plenty of jealous "obstacles" standing by to offer their unsolicited opinions.

The result of apathy and its cousins, jealousy and antagonism, is that pastors who have been play-acting are going to be brought down. Who will be lifted up? Perhaps humble, spiritually mature pastors and lay leaders who seek God, without pretense, to know

His complete forgiveness and unconditional love through humbling conviction and confession, pockets of light reflecting His presence and glory.

Walking in the Light of God's People

As each one has received a special gift, employ it in serving one another as good stewards of the manifold grace of God. (1 Peter 4:10 NASB)

Pause and consider this "manifold" or "multi-faceted" grace of God. God's grace—His unmerited favor—has been expressed to you in these different ways or facets:

- You have received God's grace as He's shown you acceptance during those times when you've failed (Romans 15:7).
- You've received God's grace when He's encouraged you when you were sad or disappointed (1 Thessalonians 5:11).
- You have received God's grace when He has supported you during times of struggle (Galatians 6:2).

Now pause and ask God: "How could I better express the glory of your grace to others?" Ask Him specifically about how to show more of His acceptance, encouragement, and support to others. Listen and be still. Allow God's Spirit to reveal the people in your life who need to receive more of His glorious grace expressed through you.

After you've heard from the Lord, complete the following sentences:

- *I could better express God's acceptance to …*
- *I could better express God's encouragement to …*
- *I could better express God's support to …*

"And let us consider one another in order to stir up love and good works" (Hebrews 10:24).

With vulnerability and sincerity, share what God has revealed to you with a partner or small group. Pray together. Ask that God's Spirit would express His grace through you, so that others would be able to see Him in you. Offer a simple prayer, such as the following:

Heavenly Father,
Please help me to be more accepting of _____.
Please show me how to do this in practical ways.

L-5 Living with a passionate longing for purity and to please Him in all things

OBSTACLE 5
UNWILLINGNESS TO BELIEVE

The need to understand God by relying on your limited, rational mind can be an obstacle to fully understanding and experiencing the Jesus-Now work of God in our time.

In my years of ministry, especially as I've marveled at how the interest and prayer for revival has grown, I've met Christians who are content to stand back and watch. Something makes them uncomfortable about revival, renewal, a "reset" of society. Their words, body language, or mere absence from spiritual gatherings say, "I just don't believe." In my opinion, there are three possible reasons why their unbelief remains an obstacle to their own spiritual awakening.

For some people, unbelief is really a reflection of their desire to "know for sure," not a rush to judge, discount, or disown something about which they don't care or want to understand.

For others, unbelief is really an unwillingness to change. Who wants to be disrupted? Why would you want spiritual awakening, an unpredictable and, in some ways, disorderly movement of God's Spirit to disrupt a comfortable pattern? No doubt a baby is more comfortable in the womb and would probably prefer to stay there than make the traumatic journey through the birth canal—even if it means new life. And for others, unbelief is a response to being convicted of unresolved sin. Finally, we must face the truth. At one time or another, this person is you and me.

Revival means admitting to God and to others that underneath the make-up and cologne, behind our bluff and boast to make others think we have it all together, we are just like Isaiah who said, "Woe to me, I am ruined." Because revival is all-too real, because the sacrifice of following Christ may seem too costly, those "on the outside looking in" may say, "I don't believe."

A QUESTION OF ATTITUDE

Over the past few years, as I've spoken to churches and parachurch ministries throughout North America, I've seen the above obstacles "come to life" in the form of attitudes in fellow believers. Like me, these are people weighed down with the baggage of original sin, who choose to keep walking, to keep following Christ. Like you and I, they know the obstacles that keep them from being open to spiritual awakening and realizing our one and only true hope in life rests in a personal relationship with Jesus Christ.

The question I've asked them is the same one I want to ask you:

How would you describe your need, your desire, your willingness to experience true spiritual awakening?

If God ever brings about another Great Awakening in our land, it will be because He moves in people like you and me, who come to Him just as we are. The way you approach the Lord may be inseparably linked to how you approach the need for awakening in your nation and in your life. The way you approach Him may be described along a continuum, a "Scale of Spiritual Awakening." Where do you find yourself along this scale?

SPIRITUAL AWAKENING SCALE: A SELF-ASSESSMENT

Antagonistic >

Does this word describe your present attitude? What are the events that have made you antagonistic to God over the past weeks, months, and years? Have you ever thought that these feelings are the very things God may use to humble you and bring you to Himself?

Antagonistic > **Indifferent**

What does this word feel like to you? Lukewarm? In-between? Is it a word that describes your present relationship with Christ? Billy Graham has suggested that it's possible to be inoculated against the gospel by receiving just a little bit of it. What is the "little" you've received? What more do you still long to know?

Antgonistic > Indifferent > **Acknowledging**

A word that says, "I know something's going on." When you read the Word and see how God has worked in people's lives, you know there's more to life than what you currently have. It's a sigh of relief that says, "I see," and a feeling of anxiousness that says, "I want more." Is that what you're acknowledging to yourself right now? You've received? What more do you still long to know?

Antagonistic > Indifferent > Acknowledging > **Seeking**

Somewhere, somehow, God broke through your obstacles,

and you've never been the same. Once you got a taste you had to have more, and so you've followed Him. Which steps of obedience have proved most costly? What steps have brought you closest to Him?

Antagonistic > Indifferent > Acknowledging > Seeking > **Involved**

The person who's involved in revival is involved in a life of selflessness. This is a daily habit of loving Jesus because He first loved you (1 John 4:19). Each day, you practice this love, a little more of you dies, and a little more of Jesus begins to live. What would this kind of intimate relationship with Christ look like? What is keeping you from praying for this kind of new awakening in your own life?

Where are you on this spectrum? Where is your heart beating in relationship to God who is awakening a nation, one life at a time? Will you be one of those people He uses?

The obstacles to revival are not insurmountable, because the true obstacle to revival is *singular*. It's me. And it's you. God doesn't want any obstacle to spiritual awakening. He just wants you and me to walk with Him every moment of every day—starting now! As that happens, as the number of footsteps in one, obedient direction increase, we will join this Jesus-Now Awakening. We will be tempted to say, "This is what it looks like!"

The surprise will be on us.

SEVEN

What Might the New Awakening Look Like?

As a child growing up on a farm in Mississippi, I was reared on anticipation. I knew the fortunes and security of my family depended on what came down from the sky—steady rain and warm sun to grow our garden, soybeans, cotton, and corn that meant food and income. Though I was only a child, I remember how all of life changed every August. Something was happening; something important that demanded the attention of everyone in our family.

The harvest was approaching.

I remember asking questions. I had a deep desire to know exactly when the harvest would be ready. This was something so momentous, so big; I wanted to be part of it.

I asked my uncle, "When is it going to happen, Uncle Millard? When will the harvest come?"

Always his response was, "Wait. Just wait, Tom. I know you're excited. I know the fields look ripe. I can't tell you when it will happen." Then he'd turn his gaze from the green, rolling fields, look into my eyes and say, "When the time comes, you and I will know it. It will be obvious."

Though I no longer live on a farm, the sense of anticipation

I felt as a child is still very much a part of who I am. As an adult, I'm still curious, still excited about the future. Today the "fields" that preoccupy me are not soybeans and cotton, but a landscape of lives, Christians from all denominations and walks of life. In my brief lifetime, I've seen this landscape of the church in various seasons of growth and seeming stagnation. In the past several years, quite frankly, a number of men and women in the church have looked withered. They seem to have lost their vitality. Some seem to have lost their will to grow.

But they are a shrinking majority. Over the past decade, something remarkable has been happening in our nation and in the church. Something has begun to change.

SUPPOSE GOD ASKS OF US ...

- Something is happening in our nation. Christians who are aware can tell it when a man named Bill McCartney gathers seventy-two men together in 1990 to seek God, and when, in four short years, that group mushrooms into stadium-sized and small group gatherings across America with an attendance totaling two hundred eighty thousand. These men have come together to ask the question, "What does it mean to honor Jesus Christ, to become a man of integrity, to become a promise keeper?"
- Something is happening to our nation when Henry Blackaby's book, *Experiencing God*, sells a record number of copies because it speaks to people about a quality and depth of relationship with the Lord for which they long.
- Something is happening to our nation when International Renewal Ministry receives dozens of requests

from pastors and church leaders across the United States and abroad who want to experience the reconciliation, the community, the unity of the Spirit that comes only through humbling confession, deep-felt conviction, and repentance.

- Something is happening not only in our nation but in Canada as well, when sixty-five thousand Christians gather simultaneously in cities across their country to pray for God to bring revival to their nation.

- Something is happening to our nation when more than a quarter of a million teenage youth willingly turn their backs on the temptation to become sexually active and instead pledge to their family and friends—most of all to God—that they'll wait and preserve that most intimate human relationship for their marriage night.

- Something is happening in our nation when a man like Bill Bright, who as founder and president of Campus Crusade for Christ International, has experienced many personally significant spiritual milestones, conducts a forty-day fast that he describes as "the greatest spiritual experience of my life."[1] When he tells seven hundred Christian leaders gathered in Orlando, Florida, "We need revival to come," then asks them to pray for two million Americans to fast forty days, I know this is not merely a dream of Bill Bright, it is the definite work of God.[2]

These are the kinds of things that cause me to sit up and take notice that something deeply profound and deeply spiritual is taking place across our country. There's something that's bringing new life to a church that's shown signs of withering. There's something that goes to the root of our need for the only One who can truly give us new life. Something that's as inevitable as rain and as necessary as harvest. Something called revival, the revival of Christ's church—a Jesus-Now Awakening where you and I will be followed by many men and women making first-time commitments to Christ.

Revival is happening this very moment in the coal-mining country of West Virginia. Prayer and desperation for God led to a great movement of God. As of May 2016, over 3,000 people in Mingo County have given their lives to Jesus Christ and been baptized. The Holy Spirit has fallen in great power over this area of our country—a dream for many who've been praying.

Katie Endicott, a young wife, mother, and teacher at Mingo Central High School recounts, "I've been overwhelmed and blessed by this revival because this community has been consecrated in prayer for generations and generations. This has been decades in the making. People like my dad, a pastor, have been waking up at 4:00 a.m. and going to the church to pray for revival." Revival is happening, it's happening now and it even has a name: "The Coalfield Revival" or the "Appalachian Awakening!"[3]

Today, when I look at the national landscape called the American church, I sense the childhood anticipation of the harvest building in me once again. Although I feel the anticipation, already I know the answer. It was the same one I heard as a farm child looking for an earlier harvest. Wait.

While I look forward to the day of revival in the United States, while I chuckle at my own insatiable desire to "know when," I wait. And I pray. My greatest prayer is that God would engulf our nation and all who claim to follow Christ in a sweeping movement of His Spirit. My prayer is that He would revive Christians, starting with me, and that this new breath of His Spirit would awaken new and old believers to a fresh, deepening love for Christ.

Walking
in the Light
of God's
Son

Do not turn your freedom into an opportunity for the flesh.
(Galatians 5:13 NASB)

As we embrace the imperative of our personal prayer for a Jesus-Now Awakening, let's quietly pray King David's prayer: "Create in me a clean heart, O God" (Psalm 51:10).

Reflect on a recent time in your life when you did *not* love others well. Share your thoughts with Jesus. Tell Him about your sadness and regret.

Lord, I know that I did not love well when ...

Now prepare for a time of cleansing and renewal with Jesus.

Lord, by your Spirit, would you remove anything from my life that hinders the expression of your love. Cleanse me, forgive me, empower me to live and love like Jesus.

W-3 Yielding to the Scripture's protective cautions
and transforming power to bring life-change in me

SPIRIT-
EMPOWERED
Faith

I know these are the prayers of many believers, men, and women who are just as eager as I am for revival to come. I know that whether they admit it or not, they live with their own questions. If you have prayed for revival, if this book has caused you to seek spiritual awakening for the first time, the same questions may be stirring inside you too. Questions such as:

- How close are we to full-fledged revival, renewal, reset?
- What will it look like personally and corporately?

- Will we know revival when it comes, as the movement takes place?
- And if so, how will we know?

What leads us to ask these questions? Is it because we're too impatient, too curious to wait? Do we want to know the exact time, size, and shape of revival because as human beings we like certainty more than mystery? Is it because we want the puzzle solved?

I believe the answer to all of the above is yes. I also believe revival is a lot like a long-awaited farm harvest—its timing is out of our hands. As Uncle Millard said, "When the time comes, you and I will know it. We'll know it. It will be obvious."

If revival does in fact come in God's own time, what are we to do in the meantime? You and I can pray that we'll be open to receive all that He has to give the church and our nation when He breathes life back into our hearts, our minds, our very being. As we wait, we can be inspired by the growing evidence of God's unfolding work in our nation. We can revel in stories like the ones you've read. We can look at these glimpses of what He's doing as snapshots—small, focused, yet important glimpses of the "big picture" of a Jesus-Now Awakening.

Let me be clear: What we're going to look at is not a window on the future. The purpose is not to assume that you or I can know what revival will look like. The goal is not to think we can sneak a peek at the Master's painting while His work is still in progress.

The goal is to know the Master Himself!

Most Christians today are unfamiliar with the big picture principles of revival. One reason is because they are unfamiliar with James Burns, a student of revival, whose book, *Revivals, Their Laws and Leaders*, is a forgotten classic. Periodically, a work is produced that transcends time. Burns' volume, written in 1909 and last published in 1960, is such a book. In his volume,

Burns identifies eleven laws or principles of revival. In no way are they similar to Finney's "Seven Indicators." These principles don't tell us what to look for. Though they're intriguing, though they draw us again and again to Scripture, they aren't clues for coming revival as much as they're foundational truths about how spiritual awakening has taken place throughout history.

THE PRINCIPLE OF EBB AND FLOW

Communication of any big truth, such as spiritual awakening, rests somewhat on an effective analogy or word picture. In illustrating revival, Burns uses the image of a wave. "Any progress (that moves us closer in our relationship toward God, [sic])," he wrote, "Is like the incoming tide. Each wave is a revival, going forward, receding, and being followed by another. To the onlooker, it seems as if nothing is gained, but the force behind the ebb and flow is the power of the tide."[4]

Think of how the "wave action" of revival makes sense.

Like a wave, our age will have its own peculiar characteristics. The activity of prayer, the turning to God that we see building gradually today, is unique from any other spiritual tide in history.

Like a wave, revival will crest at some point. The culmination will be relatively short before the wave follows its natural course and recedes. It's impossible to live "at the peak" or "on the crest" forever. A revival will move us to new heights and revitalize us. Like reaching the top of a mountain, we know our time on the summit is limited. The time comes to move on. The exhilaration of the view is what inspires us when we go back down to live in the valley. This is the ebb and flow of revival. Spiritual awakening also only lasts for a brief time, but its impact can linger much longer.

Where have you felt God at work in your own life? Is the "ebb" of being drawn back to the truth of your own broken nature or the "flow" of His unseen but very real power moving you forward to Him? Both movements are from the same loving God. "The Law (or Principle) which moves the mighty tides of the ocean," wrote Burns, "is the same which ruffles the surface of the little pool made by the rain on a summer afternoon."[5]

THE PRINCIPLE OF SPIRITUAL GROWTH

The goal of revival is not to get absorbed in guessing when the wave will start. The goal of revival is to know the Father. The goal is spiritual growth—not just growth of the individual but growth of the church toward a new level of dedication and spirituality. One of the greatest examples of this was seen in Savonarola, the noted Italian preacher of the Florentine Revival in fifteenth century Italy. As a young man, he spent hours at the altar in prayer. Burdened over the world's rejection of Christ and salvation, he fasted, prayed night and day, and poured over Scriptures.

The principle of spiritual growth is that through revival, just as in Savonarola's day, the spiritual and moral temperament of the whole community is changed.

Imagine how your own community—your church, your school, the neighborhood you call home—might be changed by a spiritual awakening. Imagine what spiritual growth could occur.

Walking
in the Light
of God's
Word

Preach the word! Be ready in season *and* out of season. Convince, rebuke, exhort, with all longsuffering and teaching. (2 Timothy 4:2)

Each of us is called to speak of the transforming power of God's Word. Pause for a moment and reflect on a favorite Bible verse or a recent devotional time in the Word. How has this truth brought change in you? How has God's Word brought more of Christ-likeness in you?

Pause to give thanks to God for this truth. Thank Him for how His truth is becoming real in you. Then ask Him: "Who might benefit from hearing me share this truth?" Is there someone at home, a friend, or colleague who needs to hear about the way God's Word has changed you?

Think about some of the contexts in which you can express Jesus and His Word to others. Could there be someone in your daily activities and relationships that could benefit from knowing some of the ways God is at work in you? Is there someone in your community of relationships who could benefit from hearing how God is changing you and then experience how you relate to them in a different way? Ask the Lord to reveal this to you, listen for His answer, and then make plans to live out what He reveals.

W-4 Humbly and vulnerably sharing of the Spirit's transforming work through the Word

SPIRIT-
EMPOWERED
Faith

THE PRINCIPLE OF PROVIDENCE/SOVEREIGNTY

Savonarola surely admitted that anything he said or did was part of God's divine plan. Because spiritual awakening occurs on God's timetable, not ours, His sovereign will always remains in charge. Like the wave action of the ocean, revival is always under His control, and for all its power, it is orderly. Even though we know His providence is at work, we can't determine exactly when the wave will hit. This is consistent with Scripture: "The secret things belong to the Lord our God" (Deuteronomy 29:29). Though we can perceive the indicators of revival—thanks to the human insights of a gifted, godly person such as Charles Finney—the sovereignty of God is the final determining factor in any revival.

Consider the time and energy you might spend on pondering the "what ifs" of revival. What would happen if you invested that same effort in considering the nature and characteristics of God? Might the way you view Him change the way you understand and view revival?

THE PRINCIPLE OF THE DRY SEASON

Look at any spiritual awakening in history, including those that have occurred in our country, and you'll discover an obvious, common thread: Revival is always preceded by spiritual deadness. It can be the lawlessness in 1800 that preceded the Cane Ridge Awakening or the indifference that defined the mood and times of New York City prior to Jeremiah Lanphier's first noontime prayer meeting in 1857.

To use the analogy of the wave action, the dry season would be the trough, the tide at its lowest ebb. This does not make the dry season any less a part of revival. God is still sovereign, still in charge. The trough is just as much a part of the wave as the whitecap.

Is it possible that the dry season of your church, your community, your nation, may be part of revival? Is it possible that, at some point, we may be coming out of that trough?

THE PRINCIPLE OF FULLNESS OF TIME

As it continues in all its "fullness," dryness always leads to desperation. Out of their profound sense of dissatisfaction, often with a certain degree of gloom, people begin to cry out to God. We call that prayer. Remember the earlier story of the Hebrides Islands in the late 1940s? A small group of men meeting in a barn began to cry out, "Oh, God, move on your people." Two women, down the road in a neighboring village, began to pray, "Oh, God, move."

They cried out because there was nowhere else to turn. Their dryness had led to desperation.

The story of the Hebrides is the story of virtually every revival. Out of a remnant, a large-scale movement is born—a movement that encompasses a large area. Strangely enough, the spiritual phenomenon that unfolds is often largely unknown! Regardless of how anonymous God's hand is, revival occurs in "the fullness of time." His people in His time demonstrate the principle of patience and faith in which the longings of God's followers are fully expressed.

Has the dry season been allowed to run its course in your life? Imagine the dry season of a nation, in the fullness of time, giving way to desperation. Imagine a remnant in our nation crying out, building momentum, leading a large-scale awakening.

THE PRINCIPLE OF LEADERSHIP

In any revival, at least one prophet always emerges. Though he or she may be a leader, the person does not "lead" revival in the classic sense of taking control and directing followers to do certain tasks. The prophetic figure in any spiritual awakening doesn't create revival; he or she *interprets* it. The prophet doesn't direct the movement; he or she *embodies* it.

In the Great Shantung Revival of 1927, a Norwegian Lutheran woman scoured the waterfront, aggravating pastors, evangelists, and missionaries by asking, "Are you born again?" Her inquisitiveness and personality happened to be the unique contribution that helped stir revival.[6]

Revival is always flavored by the unique personality and mission of the prophet. Against the materialism of his day, St. Francis of Assisi raised the voice of poverty. Out of the Welsh Revival rose the spirited devotion of lay Christians.

Yet despite all leaders' unique personalities, revival is always directed by one person—the Lord Himself. In any spiritual awakening, there is always one leader and one leader only—God. Through the Holy Spirit, chosen people embody or epitomize what He is doing for their time.

Think of the most humble, dedicated Christian you know. These qualities of devotion to God, service to others, and obedience to the Word, prayer, and sacrifice are part of the personality consistent with the people God chooses to embody spiritual awakening.

THE PRINCIPLE OF BROKENNESS AND CONFESSION

Brokenness and confession is what the prophet discovers and what the participants in revival experience. When brokenness, confession, and repentance begin to occur among God's people, revival spreads with extraordinary swiftness. As pastors are sensitized to these issues, pointed preaching begins to occur. The principle of brokenness and confession then yields to a wonderful outcome.

As a result of confession and purification of the heart, people become so magnetically attracted to Christ that their dedication grows into a great enthusiasm to follow Him. Naturally, the good news is too life-changing, too wonderful to contain. There's an enthusiasm to serve Jesus and a desire to bring others to Him. The person who experiences this new life in God wants everyone to know the One behind this new reality. This is evangelism in its most contagious form.

When have you ever found yourself so broken, so aware of your sin that the only thing you could do was come to God and confess? What do you think would happen if the genuine remorse of a few swelled and became the repentance of multiplied thousands in our country? Based on His promise to forgive, how do you suppose the lives of individuals, the life of the church, and life as a whole in our nation might change?

THE PRINCIPLE OF INFLUENCE

A by-product of evangelism supplies one more principle in the natural development of spiritual awakening. As revival progresses—as the wave action builds, as the movement of God crests—large numbers of people discover what only a remnant once knew: Jesus Christ is alive! The influence of revival, however, is not limited merely to a spiritual plane. Awakenings have always spilled over beyond the borders of the church into the life of their towns and cities.

From the time of Hezekiah to the time of John and Charles Wesley in England, revival's influence is always felt in the political and social structure. When revival comes, the church takes on a new role in society; clergy gain new respect. As revived Christians actually live like Christ, they reach out to their schools, workplaces, and neighborhoods in what some would label "social action."

Can you think of a time when the influence of one person changed an entire group? Think of the greatest social movement of your generation. Then consider that this show of force is only a fraction of the power and influence that could result when God ignites and sustains a movement of His own.

THE PRINCIPLE OF VARIETY

No two spiritual awakenings are exactly alike. While some of their characteristics will be *similar*, the actual expression of each movement is unique to its own era. In fact, each revival's emphasis is, in many ways, a reaction against the prevailing winds of the day. For instance, Charles Finney's preaching on a Christian's responsibility to conform, confess, and receive Christ came in reaction to the hyper-Calvinism that maintained all had been decided beforehand by God, that your salvation or its absence was decided before you were born. The Moravian movement of the eighteenth century was a pendulum swing away from the cold residue of the Reformation.

What things are unique about the age in which we live? What is special about the social climate, the problems, or sins that trouble you, as a Christian? Can you name some fellow believers who share your views?

THE PRINCIPLE OF RECOIL

In an unforced, almost natural manner, revival runs its course. Any movement that strikes in one direction creates a reciprocal reaction. If the church is under a heavy hand of authority, the revival will bring freedom as with the Wesley Revival. If the church has become so free that it is licentious, the revival will bring authority as it did in the Reformation. The principle of recoil then takes effect. As Burns summed it up, "Every revival has a time limit. It has its day, and then it recedes."[7] After the wave crests and impacts the shore, the ebb begins. The prophetic "leader" passes on. The truth endures; the fervor fades.Through the principle of recoil, two things can then happen. The first is that spiritual awakening receives some kind of negative reaction. After the Welsh Revival, a reactionary named J. B. Morgan tried to debunk what God had done by revealing that five years after a hundred thousand had come to Christ, "only" eighty thousand remained.

A second characteristic of recoil is that with awakening, corruption can also come. The reputation of poverty in the early Franciscan movement, for example, gave way eventually to the people's lust for money.

How large, how significant would revival need to be in this country for the recoil of negativity and corruption to surface? Imagine how powerful and life-changing (threatening to some) a spiritual awakening would be to cause others to rise up in dismay and disbelief because of personal and national sins.

THE PRINCIPLE OF DOCTRINE

Always, after spiritual wakening runs its God-appointed course, church doctrine moves back to simplicity. This is especially true if the message of the gospel has been forgotten or overlaid with theology or tradition. Whatever the revival, the message of the cross has always become central.

Whenever people are moved to know and follow Him, they step up to the reality of their sin and come face-to-face with the only One who can make the necessary sacrifice—Jesus, who overcame death for us on the cross and through the resurrection. Revival makes all other issues secondary.

What is the one doctrine, one truth in your life that would cause you to pray for revival? When all that is secondary falls away, what is the one central fact of Christianity upon which your faith and the hope of this nation rests?

Walking
in the Light
of God's
People

So we are Christ's ambassadors; God is making his appeal through us.
We speak for Christ when we plead, "Come back to God!" (2 Corinthians 5:20 NLT)

Pause quietly before the Lord and ask God to bring a name or face to your mind. Ask God to speak to you about someone who needs to en-counter a compassionate ambassador. Ask God to show you a person who might need your demonstration of His forgiveness, acceptance, compassion, kindness, or support.

Lord, I sense it is important for me to share your love with

_____.

Now ask yourself: How am I going to live as Christ's ambassador? And where am I going to get the power to live a life of caring for others?

The power to demonstrate Christ's love will only come through the constraining love of Jesus and His demonstration of love *for* you (2 Corinthians 5:14). The only hope you have of becoming an effective ambassador of Jesus is to experience more and more of the love He has for you, so you'll be equipped to love others.

Pause to pray with a partner or small group. Thank God that He has loved you with an everlasting love that will be the source of giving to others. Ask the Holy Spirit to engage you and empower you as you share Jesus with others.

M-1 Imparting the gospel and one's very life in daily activities, relationships, vocation, and community

WHERE NOW?

As you consider these principles of revival and as you relate them to your own life, with what are you left?

- A sense of expectancy for spiritual awakening in your lifetime?
- A new conviction of your brokenness?
- A new awareness of our nation's ungodly ways?
- A new love for Jesus?

I hope by now you have a much better understanding and deeper appreciation for what revival is and how it develops, builds, crests, and recedes in God's own time. I hope the wave you're able to picture is more than just a convenient way to think about the last time you enjoyed a warm, sunny beach. I hope Burns' analogy has carried you close to the real impact revival has made in history and the life-changing force it will one day bring again.

Seen as a whole, these timeless principles offer more than just the "big picture" of spiritual awakening. As you look at each truth, the real discovery is to see the character of God:

- In the *ebb and flow* of revival is God's unseen power to move toward us and work through us in His season and for His reasons.
- In the *goal* of revival is God's constant desire for us to grow as His church.
- In the *unknown timetable* of revival is God's providence and sovereignty.
- In the *dry season* that precedes revival is God's reminder that without Him we are spiritually dead.
- In the *fullness of time,* when our dryness leads to desperation, is God's faithfulness to hear our prayers.
- In the *"leadership"* of revival are God's purposes and plans embodied in His chosen men and women.
- In the *brokenness and confession* of revival is God's life-saving, life-renewing grace of Christ, offered in a way we can best receive it—on our knees.
- In the *influence* of revival is God's unique flair for using unique individuals to meet the unique needs of the time.

- In the *recoil* of revival is God's infinite ability to work through those who turn their back on Him, even if they claim to be His followers.
- In the *doctrine* of revival is God's heart—His Son, Jesus Christ—whose life, death, and resurrection are the pulse of every awakening, including the one that awaits us.

When you see God through these principles, you're seeing revival for what it truly is—a revitalized relationship with Jesus Christ that comes to life in the presence of His reawakened church, a renewed vessel commissioned to help others know Him. When knowing Him is your personal prayer, revival stops being theoretical and starts becoming deeply personal. When you realize that His Spirit has moved powerfully in history, when you acknowledge He can move again, you can let go of wondering what the next revival will look like or when it will come. When you let the principles reflect a person, you will find yourself thanking Him, praising Him, seeking Him, loving Him. That's when you will find yourself waiting on the Lord, praying for His people to be renewed in His time.

Of course, as we find renewed spiritual life, we'll be magnetically drawn to our friends who don't know Christ. We'll naturally introduce them to the greatest friend of all, thus issuing in what could be the most productive period of evangelism in the history of our world. This result of revival is the ultimate goal of God's own heart and the penultimate reason for revival—the Creator recreating and building His kingdom on earth prior to ushering in His eternal kingdom.

"I sense a strong unifying force among denominational and parachurch ministries across our land for strategic revival and renewal," says Kay Horner, National Cry Out America Coordinator and Executive Director of Awakening America Alliance.

Involving more than fifty partnering ministries, AAA's mission is serving kingdom initiatives for spiritual awakening and missional living, while providing a broad umbrella under which the body of Christ in the United States can unite together in seeking revival.

Spearheaded by Awakening America Alliance, National Prayer Committee, and One Cry, numerous denominational and parachurch ministries have united their efforts to reestablish the National Prayer Accord. The Prayer Accord helps unite Jesus-followers in seeking the face of God through prayer and fasting, persistently asking our Father to send revival to the church and spiritual awakening to our nation so that Christ's Great Commission might be fulfilled worldwide in our generation.

In the words of AAA strategic prayer partner Doug Small, who speaks from more than twenty years leadership in the prayer movement, "The core issue revolves around love. In America, we have a fundamental loss of passion and recognition of how much God loves us and what He's done for us. Our true motivation should be 'If you love me ... '. It is my own personal relationship with God that motivates me to love, care, and share with others. Consequently, we understand a National Prayer Accord is neither the harmony nor the melody; it is the ongoing cadence on which the harmony and the melody ride."

David Franklin, who coordinates an expanding network of pastors in Bartow County, Georgia, northwest of Atlanta, sees a new, growing unity in the church. "God is bringing His body together across racial and denominational lines. In our region, a hundred churches—from evangelical to Pentecostal and charismatic—are working together and praying together. As Henry Blackaby has said so well, revival is not limited to one church or denomination."[8]

Franklin, along with his fellow pastors and their congregations, has already caught a powerful glimpse of the emerging revival. In April 2011, vicious tornadoes with sustained 190-mile-per-hour winds ripped through Tuscaloosa and Birmingham, Alabama, killing sixty-four people and causing $2.4 billion of damage.

"On Saturday morning, I was told to come to a meeting with state and county emergency management leaders. The first words they said to me were, 'You're in charge of tornado recovery.' I thought they were joking. They weren't." In the midst of this incredible moment, Franklin pointed out, "When the government starts coming to the church for help, that's a good sign that God is on the move."

Franklin went on to say: "Revival reveals the absolute holiness of God. When His people are in unity (Psalm 133), God commands His blessing. In revival, we will not touch the glory, and we will not take credit. We, as the Lord's followers, are to continue to walk in humility. The Lord, alone, takes all the credit."[9]

The call to revival means coming to God daily just as you are. Coming to Him with all your baggage, knowing that He already knows what you're carrying inside. It means coming to Him as one who's been "damaged in shipment." It means coming as a broken vessel in need of repair, a vessel that needs to be reshaped because it's the only way to be strong enough to resist the hard knocks that the days ahead are sure to bring.

The call to revival is the call to come home:

- Come home from your impossible schedule that has left you out of breath and out of touch with God.
- Come home from the trivial diversions that have robbed you of time with the Lord.
- Come home from loud radio commercials, loud television shows, and other mindless chatter that keeps you from hearing God's still, small voice.

The call to awakening is a call to come to God as a child who has wandered from his or her loving parent. The call to spiritual awakening is to all believers who want to know they are forgiven, accepted, and loved again—*as if for the first time.*

Today a few people in our land have heard this call to a Jesus-Now Awakening. They are the ones who have been gripped by conviction, confession, and repentance. They are the men and women coming home to the Father they had once forgotten, ignored, or for whom they've simply been too busy. They are like a remnant in a dry season crying, "Oh, God, move. Move in my nation. Move in *me!*"

Is this your voice? Is this your prayer?

Do you want to know what it feels like to be alive again?

Would you like to come home? Are you already standing on the doorstep to your part in this Jesus-Now Awakening?

EIGHT

The Most Important
Decision of All

The harbingers of this Jesus-Now revival are all around us. The evidence is unavoidable.

Within three weeks after I returned from Orlando, Florida, where nearly seven hundred Christian leaders had prayed and fasted three days for our nation, I saw a lead article in *National & International Religion Report*. For years, I had been praying for revival in our nation. In Orlando, the voice of revival was coming through loud and clear:

- "God is calling the Church to a time of consecrated prayer and fasting," said Thomas Trask, the general superintendent of the Assemblies of God at the time. This is "the beginning of what has to happen."[1]
- When revival comes, "sinners will race to the Church instead of the Church racing to save sinners," said author and presenter on revival, Nancy Leigh DeMoss.[2]
- Broadcaster Pat Robertson commented, "God is visiting the earth."[3]
- David Bryant of Concerts of Prayer International said fasting is not an end in itself but involves setting

aside our "ordinary way of living, because something extraordinary is about to happen."[4]

Dr. David McKenna, President Emeritus of Asbury Seminary, has noticed a changing, deepening spiritual climate on college campuses. Since writing *The Coming Great Awakening* in 1990, he has become more convinced than ever that America is ripe for spiritual awakening and that young people, college-aged and under, will play a key role. "Wherever I've spoken, whether it's Gordon College, Messiah College, Houghton College, or others, I've met a core group of students who are meeting and praying for revival on their campus."[5]

In the aftermath of Ferguson, Missouri, which had been a blistering cauldron of racial strife, small yet significant works of healing were emerging. In an online blog for the Billy Graham Evangelistic Association, Krisy Etheridge wrote:

The day before Thanksgiving 2014, a team of crisis-trained Billy Graham Rapid Response Team chaplains arrived in Ferguson, Missouri. They were responding to rioting and unrest in the wake of a grand jury's decision not to indict police officer Darren Wilson for fatally shooting eighteen-year-old Michael Brown. While many of the chaplains have served in the aftermath of hurricanes, tornadoes and other disasters, they didn't know what to expect in Ferguson, where buildings are burned or boarded up and tensions are running high. What they found was a city searching for hope, open to those willing to get their hands dirty and help.

When the chaplains arrived early Tuesday, they noticed a pickup truck was parked in their usual spot. Chaplain Kevin Williams recognized the driver as a young man he had spoken with earlier. Jeff Naber, manager of chaplain development and ministry relations relates what happened. "The young man told Kevin, 'Man, I haven't slept all night. I kept on thinking about what you told me—about God and God's love and eternal life.'"

The man told Kevin he wanted to pray to receive Jesus as his Savior, and he did. But he didn't want to keep it to himself. He immediately drove home, picked up his girlfriend and brought her to meet the chaplains. She listened to her boyfriend explain what his decision meant to him, and with tears in her eyes, she prayed to accept Christ, too.[6]

If spiritual awakening is a thunderous roar of the Spirit, the accounts in this book speak of revival's loud whispers. They may not be audible where you worship or live, but they are real. And by all indications, these heart-cries for God are growing.

Walking
in the Light
of God's
Word

Proverbs 3:32 (NIV) reminds us that the Lord "takes the upright into his confidence." Can you remember a time when you have sensed that the Lord has taken you into His confidence? Reflect on some of your own times with the Lord. It may have been while reading the Scriptures, praying, talking with another believer, singing songs of worship, or even just listening to His voice. Can you remember a moment when you experienced an almost tangible moment with God?

I remember having a personal encounter with God when ...

- He drew me close to Him by ...
- He gave me specific direction about ...

- He provided a warning about …
- He revealed Himself as …
- He confronted me concerning …
- He affirmed my …
- He reassured me about …

Share prayers of thanksgiving with a partner or small group. Celebrate that He has revealed Himself to you and then pray with confidence that He will do it again. Ask Him boldly to take you into His confidence again! *Speak, Lord. I am listening* …

L-2 Listening to and hearing God for direction and discernment

Even during the writing of this book, the evidence for revival in our nation continues to grow. There will be more stories, more accounts, and more examples of broken, changed lives, all of which will have one explanation: Only an extraordinary work of the Holy Spirit could bring this about.

Today, a great turning is taking place, a turning called repentance.

Repentance involves turning from sin and turning to Jesus. Turning from sin happens simultaneously as we turn toward the One who took upon Himself your sin, my sin—the One in whom we now live as a new creation in Christ (2 Corinthians 5:17). Think of repentance as both *confession* (to agree with God), and *conviction* (to see as God sees). Repentance, then, is nothing less than a life-changing turning point in a new, now-and-forever relationship with Jesus Christ.

As Christians, continue to fast and pray, asking yourself,

"What do I believe about spiritual awakening in me and in my nation?" As you explore this question, I suspect you'll find yourself in one of three "places" regarding revival:

- *You may be one who's already experienced a personal revival.* Your life may have ebbed until you could do nothing more than come to God out of desperation as your last and only hope. For you, revival is real because you've rediscovered that God is real and alive. No wonder you're praying for awakening to come to your nation, your church, and your friends. You've been brought back to life!

- *You may still feel like someone "on the outside looking in."* Spiritual awakening has not been part of your spiritual journey with God. Though you can't deny the power of God in the people and groups you've met in these pages, though you share the same Lord, though you pray and seek to follow His call, revival is still "out there." You're not sure whether spiritual awakening will ever be real in your life—though you're not closing the door, either.

- *You find yourself still one of the curious.* For you, spiritual awakening is neither immediately real, nor is it something you choose to discount or ignore. You're open to whatever God might show you. Praying for revival, talking to others, and searching the Scriptures to see how God has awakened others, are not out of the question. In fact, already you find yourself moving in that direction.

Regardless of where you find yourself concerning spiritual awakening, you can prepare yourself for revival. As you do, you may discover you're part of a global phenomenon that could have its birthright here in this country. Let me leave you with a concluding story.

THE STRATEGIC CONTINENT

In 1984, I felt as if I were standing at a crossroads in my life. As a Crusade Director and Director of Counseling and Follow-Up Administration for Mr. Graham, I had been working in Australia and had come to Bristol, England, for the first evangelistic meeting of six Billy Graham crusades called "Mission England." Something had been stirring in me for weeks—a desire to work overseas in evangelism. I went to Walter Smyth, the Director of International Crusades, and told him about my interest. Though my words surprised him, he was open to my request. My boss at the time, Charlie Riggs, said assuredly, "If God wants you to work overseas, that's fine with me."

When I woke up the next morning, I felt a sense of total gloom. In asking to shift my ministry area from Counseling and Follow-Up to International Ministries, I knew I had done the wrong thing, but I didn't know why. That morning I went back to Walter Smyth, feeling very chagrined. "Please, erase my request from your mind," I said.

I knew I was called to keep working in North America. I knew there was something inside me, something of God that drew me to serve people beyond my own continent. These two assurances lived within me. Sometimes, I agonized about it. Often, I prayed, "Lord, you know I desire to see people come to you. You've given me a heart for revival; You've given me a heart for yourself. Then why am I so unsettled?"

Charlie Riggs, my spiritual mentor, colleague, and close friend, knew my heart. Out of love, he began to give me overseas assignments. Out of one of these "foreign duties," I experienced a watershed moment of understanding, not only for what God was doing in my life, but for what He's doing today to bring revival to our nation and our world.

The breakthrough came in April 1986. I was busily preparing program materials for "Amsterdam '86," a rare gathering of ten thousand itinerant evangelists from around the world. I found myself hopscotching across Latin America, North America, and Asia to arrange the translation, writing, and publication of ministry guides. In between phone calls and ticket windows, I continued to pray, "Lord, you know my heart for revival. What does this work, this particular time in my life, have to do with fulfilling the desire you've given me?"

Riding in a cab through a noisy, congested section of Seoul, South Korea, I received my answer. Though I don't pretend to quote God, His voice at that particular moment was crystal clear:

Do Koreans live in North America?

"Yes," I said.

Do Latin Americans live in North America?

"Yes," I said.

Do Europeans live in North America?

Again, I said, "Yes."

For several city blocks, it was as if God read me a roll call of nations. He brought to mind nearly every continent or country I had ever visited, or knew existed. That afternoon my understanding of my own continent, my own country, changed. Though I was well aware that the United States had become the melting pot for the world's races, geography and ministry converged in my heart like a grand "Aha!" *Virtually every race, every people, every ethnic group could be found in North America. When revival comes to North America, people from all lands will carry the movement of God to their own people groups.*

I filed this realization away under "God's calling." From

month to month over the next eight years, I took it off the shelf, opened my heart to God, and asked Him, "What does this mean? I believe you've made North America a strategic part of your plan to bring others to yourself—but how? And what, if anything at all, are you calling me to do?"

In the spring of 1994, I learned the answer. The time had come for me to leave the Billy Graham Evangelistic Association. After twenty years, I had been able to invest myself in some very able partners in ministry. One was Rick Marshall, whom God had "awakened" at the Pastors' Prayer Summit at Cannon Beach, Oregon.

Out of three possible options, one rose to the top, a ministry I had been aware of for years: International Students, Incorporated (ISI). After ten weeks of prayer and interviews, I accepted the board's offer to become ISI's new president. Their mission rang true: "ISI exists to share Christ's love with international students, and to equip them for effective service in cooperation with the local church and others."

After just a few weeks on the job, I came face-to-face with these words and their meaning for revival today. I met Abel, a student from southeastern China, who was completing a PhD in computer science. He had married an American woman. Both were vivacious Christians and Bible teachers as a part of ISI's ministry at Midwestern University. Abel's coming to America, and the courageous steps he and his wife soon planned to take, were a mini-glimpse at our world's current revival stirrings.

When Abel came to the United States six years earlier, he had been a Communist. For six lonely months, he had sought friends and found none. Through the love of an International Student Friendship Partner, Abel learned about Jesus Christ, and after several years of searching and study, he gave his life to the Lord.

He married and determined not to return to China. However, as he continued to study God's Word, his own spiritual life deepened. The hope and power of the gospel were too great to ignore or to keep to himself. Abel decided he had to return to his homeland. He wanted his people to discover, to meet, and to love the Jesus he had come to know.

Abel and his wife knew when they arrived in China, they would encounter resistance, rejection, and possible persecution from their families and friends. To those who have never heard the name "Jesus" or never seen a Bible, the message of salvation could be an affront as well as the only answer to every person's search for meaning, purpose, and direction in life—*if they respond positively to Christ as Lord and Savior.* Some would be able to know life in all its abundance because they would see Christ alive in Abel and his wife. They would know eternal life because these two people, awakened by the Holy Spirit, were eager to reproduce themselves spiritually.

Abel and his wife were not alone. Suresh was a young man from India also serving with ISI. His life's desire is to help international students now in the United States go back to their respective homes and carry the same Jesus he's met to their own people.

Connie (which is not her real name) from South Africa was one of her country's educational leaders. She came to the United States to get her master's degree in education. Although she came as a nominal Christian, through vibrant believers in an international setting, her spirit, her meaning for living, was revived. Now she's going back to South Africa, not only to help her people become more educated, but also to help her people know Christ in a vital, real way.

There's a reason why Abel, Suresh, and Connie came to our

continent, our country. *Today, the world has come to North America.* The thousands of men and women from nations around the globe who are studying in America's colleges and universities—studying to become leaders in industry, science, education, and politics, eager and talented men and women—are open to explore and embrace the gospel of Jesus Christ.

It's clear to me that God brings people like Abel, Suresh, and Connie to North America for a reason. As the next Jesus-Now Awakening takes place in North America—as God's work in areas of conviction, confession, and repentance eventually builds and crests in a wave of revival—it will be obvious to all who are awakened by God, *including internationals and international students!* In turn, they will be vessels through which God will spread the truth of His Son to their respective peoples.

These are the individuals who are meeting Christ today and who will take Him back home to their respective nations, not necessarily as pastors, but as influential leaders in business, politics, education, science, and industry. By awakening the church in North America, God will be awakening the entire world through women and men who will go back to their homelands with a new message of vital spiritual life and salvation.

The current revival stirrings on our continent and in our nation do not rest with a single ministry, a gifted visionary, or the most dedicated layperson. The Jesus-Now Awakening rests with God alone. Like the tide whose ebb and flow is beyond our control, the Lord who created oceans and who changes lives will revive our nation—in His own time. God's sovereignty is for certain. And so is something else: the certainty of His Word and the power of believing prayer.

Walking in the Light of God's People

If you ask anything in My name, I will do *it*. (John 14:14)

With a partner or in a small group, pause for a few moments and ask the Lord to make this Bible promise very real. Make the request below and believe that Jesus will make it so.

Lord Jesus, I claim the promise that you are with me always (Matthew 28:20), and I make this request—certain that it is according to your will. I ask that you lead me and empower me to do my part in the Jesus-Now Awakening. I claim the promise of John 14:14—certain that you will do this because it is according to your will.

L-8 Disciplined, bold and believing prayer

SPIRIT-EMPOWERED *Faith*

"TRULY, GOD IS IN YOUR MIDST"

Charles Nuckolls, Department Chair in Anthropology at Brigham Young University, has said, "We've stripped away what our ancestors saw as essential—the importance of religion and family." He's referring to Americans in general, but he might as well have been talking about Christians hungry for a God they once knew when he says, "People feel they want something they've lost, and they don't remember what it is they've lost. But it has left a gaping hole." [7]

"That, in essence," the article concludes, "is the seeker's quest: to fill the hole with a new source of meaning. Why are we here? What is the purpose of our existence? The answers change in each generation, but the questions are eternal."[8]

We in the church believe that a personal relationship with God through Jesus Christ is the only true answer that can satisfy these eternal questions. If we expect Him to revive our spirits, if we expect God to stir us to new life, we must be willing to let Him begin the process of personal revival where He must—with all that is dead inside us. The process will not be easy.

In her closing address, "A Special Call to Prayer & Fasting for Our Country," Nancy Leigh DeMoss invited everyone in attendance in Orlando to take a good hard look past the façade of today's church to the spiritual interior of our very being, where true personal and national revival starts:

Is it possible that Jesus has lost His place in the Church? On the face of things it would not seem so. We still have prayers and preaching. We still have crosses on our church buildings. Yet, I'm reminded of the Old Testament passage in which God took His Prophet Ezekiel on a tour of the temple. In a vision, God showed His servant a hole in the wall of that temple and said, "Ezekiel, look inside the hole and see what is really going on inside." What Ezekiel saw behind the façade of spirituality was unspeakable filth, idolatry, and immorality right in the temple of God. The glory of God had departed from the Holy of Holies, and yet God's people, assured by their leaders that everything was fine, continued right on with their religious routines, programs, and practices, totally oblivious to the fact that they had lost the manifest presence of God in their midst (Ezekiel 8).

I wonder if we could get honest enough to let God tear a hole in the wall of our modern-day, respectable Christianity. Could we be honest enough to let Him tear a hole in the wall of our ministries and, even more personally, in the wall of our own hearts so we could see what's really inside?

Oh, for the presence and the power of God! You see, revival is just that sovereign act of God that restores the Lord Jesus to His rightful place as the Lord and the lover of His people. And when the glory of God fills His temple once again, then we will experience what Paul wrote about in 1 Corinthians 14, when lost people will come into our midst and the secrets of their hearts will be laid bare and they will fall on their faces and worship God and say "Truly, God is in your midst."

Revival is not just another emphasis to add to our already overcrowded agendas. It's not an option. It's not just a nice idea. A meeting with God in genuine revival is our only hope. We know that revival is a sovereign work of God, that it cannot be manufactured, that the wind blows as the Spirit directs, that He moves in His way and in His time. But I believe, as someone once said, "Set our sails to catch the winds from heaven—when God chooses to blow upon His people."[9]

One of James Burns' revival principles, the "Principle of Doctrine," reminds us that God's sovereign, spiritual awakening will take us to the centrality and simplicity of the cross. All that we can't understand about how or when God will bring revival hangs on a tree at Calvary, with a dying man brought to life again in three days.

In the resurrected Christ, the new, spiritual awakening

which our nation, church, you, and I so desperately need has already begun.

"How do you start a revival?" someone once asked the British evangelist, Gipsy Smith. He replied, "If you want to start a revival, go home, and get a piece of chalk. Go into your closet and draw a circle on the floor. Kneel down in the middle of the circle and ask God to start a revival inside the chalk mark. When He has answered your prayer, the revival has begun."[10]

Most people think that God can start a revival anytime He wishes. Can He? Will He? The Bible defines active sin in this way: "If anyone, then, knows the good they ought to do and doesn't do it, it is sin for them" (James 4:17 NIV). If God could start a revival anytime He wanted (as if we were robots), and He *isn't* doing it, or if He's holding back revival from a nation, then He would be guilty of omission by His own principles!

This Jesus-Now Revival has erupted throughout our nation whenever people have turned themselves to God in godly repentance and humility, weeping over and asking forgiveness for their sins and their selfish lives. This is spiritual awakening—to be a true follower of Christ living in a continual state of revival as a clean vessel for His service. To get a grasp of God in Spirit and in truth, and then live it, is to know revival—to know *Christ*—personally.

This is the most important decision of all: Will you choose to seek Him, to love Him, and to follow Him? Are you open to the Jesus-Now Awakening that God wants to bring about *in you*?

Walking
in the Light
of God's
Son

The sheep hear his voice, and he calls his own sheep by name.
(John 10:3 NASB)

Pause for the next few moments and ask God's Spirit to bring insight and direction concerning God's divine calling for your life. Claim this promise: "Call to Me, and I will answer you" (Jeremiah 33:3).

Quietly ask the Lord: *Why am I here? What special purpose do you have for me in this Jesus-Now Awakening? What specific calling do you have for my life?*

Now listen to the Lord. Celebrate that He longs to involve you and share these things with you, so that others might come to follow Him.

M-9 Pouring our life into others, making disciples who in turn make disciples of others

SPIRIT-
EMPOWERED
Faith

NINE

Preparing for Personal Revival

Neither you nor I can create revival, but we can pray and prepare. Like Hezekiah who sought the Lord, you can come to God just as you are with everything that concerns you, saddens you, and moves you about the condition of our nation today. You can prepare yourself for your own personal revival by asking yourself some very basic questions that follow, courtesy of Byron Paulus, Executive Director/President, Life Action Ministries. Treat them as a kind of "personal inventory of the heart," *your* heart. How do you feel toward God and all that He can and will do through you in the coming days?

Before you look at these questions, take to heart these simple suggestions:

- *Pray the prayer of the psalmist:* "Search me, O God, and know my heart; Try me, and know my anxieties; And see if *there is any* wicked way in me, and lead me in the way everlasting" (Psalm 139:23–24).
- *Be totally honest* as you answer each question.
- *Agree with God* about each need He reveals in your life. Confess each sin, with the willingness to make it right and forsake it.

- *Praise God* for His cleansing and forgiveness.
- *Renew your mind and rebuild your life* through meditation and practical application of the Word of God.
- *Review these questions* periodically to remain sensitive to your need for ongoing revival.

I've grouped the questions in key categories to help focus their impact:

GENUINE SALVATION

"Therefore, if anyone *is* in Christ, *he is* a new creation; old things have passed away; behold, all things have become new" (2 Corinthians 5:17).

1. Was there ever a time in my life that I genuinely repented of my sin?
2. Was there ever a time in my life that I placed my trust in Jesus Christ alone to save me?
3. Was there ever a time in my life that I completely surrendered to Jesus Christ as the Master and Lord of my life?

GOD'S WORD

"Oh, how I love your law! It is my meditation all the day. Your promises have been thoroughly tested, and your servant loves them" (Psalm 119:97, 140 NIV).

1. Do I love to read and meditate on the Word of God?
2. Are my personal devotions consistent and meaningful?
3. Do I practically apply God's Word to my everyday life?

Who do you say that I am? (Matthew 16:15 NASB)

Take time now to meditate on Jesus. Imagine the picture of the resurrected Christ. Use your imagination to see Jesus; see His nail-pierced hands and feet or His glorified and resurrected body. Imagine that Christ asks you this question: "Who do you say that I am?"

Quietly whisper your response: *You are my Lord, and I long to know you.*

Now ask Jesus: *What other priorities, activities, or things do I need to let go, so that I might know you more?*

Listen for His Spirit to speak.

"But whatever things were gain to me, those things I have counted as loss for the sake of Christ" (Philippians 3:7 NASB).

Yield to the Lord and surrender these things to Him. Count them as loss. Tell Jesus about your willingness to let go of the things He has revealed. For example:

Jesus, my success and career are nothing in comparison to you. My possessions and status mean nothing in light of you.

Make your declaration according to Philippians 3:8:

"I count all things to be loss in view of the surpassing value of knowing Christ Jesus my Lord" (NASB).

M-3 Championing Jesus as the only hope of eternal life and abundant living

HUMILITY

"For thus says the High and Lofty One who inhabits eternity, whose name *is* Holy: 'I dwell in the high and holy *place*, with him *who* has a contrite and humble spirit, to revive the spirit of the humble, and to revive the heart of the contrite ones'" (Isaiah 57:15).

1. Am I quick to recognize and agree with God in confession when I have sinned?
2. Am I quick to admit to others when I am wrong?
3. Do I rejoice when others are praised and recognized but my accomplishments go unnoticed by others?
4. Do I esteem all others as better than myself?

OBEDIENCE

"Obey those who rule over you, and be submissive, for they watch out for your souls, as those who must give account. Let them do so with joy and not with grief, for that would be unprofitable for you" (Hebrews 13:17).

1. Do I consistently obey what I know God wants me to do?
2. Do I consistently obey the human authorities God has placed over my life (those who do not contradict God's moral law)?

PURE HEART

"If we confess our sins, He is faithful and just to forgive us *our* sins and to cleanse us from all unrighteousness" (1 John 1:9).

1. Do I confess my sins specifically?
2. Do I keep "short sin accounts" with God (confess and forsake as He convicts)?
3. Am I willing to give up all sin for God?

CLEAR CONSCIENCE

"So I strive always to keep my conscience clear before God and man" (Acts 24:16 NIV).

1. Do I consistently seek forgiveness from those I wrong or offend?
2. Is my conscience clear with every person? (Can I honestly say, "There is no one I have ever wronged or offended in any way and not gone back to them and sought their forgiveness and made it right?")

PRIORITIES

"But seek first the kingdom of God and His righteousness, and all these things shall be added to you" (Matthew 6:33).

1. Does my schedule reveal that God is first in my life?
2. Does my checkbook reveal that God is first in my life?
3. Next to my relationship with God, is my relationship with my family my highest priority?

VALUES

"Therefore, as God's chosen people, holy and dearly loved, clothe yourselves with compassion, kindness, humility, gentleness and patience" (Colossians 3:12 NIV).

1. Do I love what God loves and hate what God hates?
2. Do I value highly the things that please God (e.g., giving, witnessing to those without Christ, studying His Word, prayer, helping, and serving others)?
3. Are my affections and goals fixed on others and eternal values?

Walking
in the Light
of God's
People

For the sorrow that is according to
the will of God produces a repentance.
(2 Corinthians 7:10 NASB)

Quietly consider this question: What deepened work of Christ-likeness might be needed in your life? Is there a work of humility, obedience, purity, forgiveness, or grace that's needed in you? Does the Lord need to do a work in your priorities, habits, or values?

Say just a sentence or two of prayerful repentance:

Change me, Lord. I want to become more like you. By your Spirit, make me more humble, obedient, forgiving, attentive, gracious, and pure of heart. I want to reflect more and more of Jesus. Change me.

Now, share your areas of needed change and repentance with a partner or small group. Allow others to pray with you and for you. Listen as another believer asks, in faith, that these changes become true in your life. Give God praise, as the Holy Spirit brings a Jesus-Now Awakening to each of your lives!

Finally, claim the promise of Scripture: Your encounter with Jesus and expression of godly sorrow will bring change to your life.

God, I believe that I will see changes in my life because of my encounter with Jesus. I look forward to seeing these changes because of my encounter with Him. I'm specifically anticipating that God will change me/my ...

W-7 A life-explained as one of "experiencing Scripture"

SPIRIT-
EMPOWERED
Faith

SACRIFICE

"But what things were gain to me, these I have counted loss for Christ" (Philippians 3:7).

1. Am I willing to sacrifice whatever is necessary to see God move in my life and church (time, convenience, comfort, reputation, pleasure, etc.)?
2. Is my life characterized by genuine sacrifice for the cause of Christ, for righteousness and justice?

SPIRIT CONTROL

"But the fruit of the Spirit is love, joy, peace, longsuffering, kindness, goodness, faithfulness, gentleness, self-control. Against such there is no law. And those *who are* Christ's have crucified the flesh with its passions and desires. If we live in the Spirit, let us also walk in the Spirit. Let us not become conceited, provoking one another, envying one another" (Galatians 5:22–26).

1. Am I allowing Jesus to be Lord of every area of my life?
2. Am I allowing the Holy Spirit to "fill" my life each day?
3. Is there consistent evidence of the fruit of the Spirit being produced in my life?

FIRST LOVE

"For to me, to live *is* Christ, and to die *is* gain. ... For I am hard-pressed between the two, having a desire to depart and be with Christ, *which is* far better" (Philippians 1:21, 23).

1. Am I as much in love with Jesus as I have ever been?
2. Am I thrilled with Jesus, filled with His joy and peace, and making Him the continual object of my love?

MOTIVES

"But Peter and the *other* apostles answered and said: 'We ought to obey God rather than men'" (Acts 5:29).

1. Am I more concerned about what God thinks about my life than about what others think?
2. Would I pray, read my Bible, give, and serve as much if nobody but God ever noticed?
3. Am I more concerned about pleasing God than I am about being accepted and appreciated by others?

MORAL PURITY

"But among you there must not be even a hint of sexual immorality, or of any kind of impurity, or of greed, because these are improper for God's holy people. Nor should there be obscenity, foolish talk or coarse joking, which are out of place, but rather thanksgiving" (Ephesians 5:3–4 NIV).

1. Do I keep my mind free from books, magazines, or entertainment that could stimulate ungodly fantasizing or thoughts that are not morally pure?
2. Are my conversation and behavior pure and above reproach?

FORGIVENESS

"Therefore, as *the* elect of God, holy and beloved, put on tender mercies, kindness, humility, meekness, longsuffering; bearing with one another, and forgiving one another, if anyone has a complaint against another; even as Christ forgave you, so you also *must do*" (Colossians 3:12–13).

1. Do I seek to resolve conflicts in relationships as soon as possible?
2. Am I quick to forgive those who wrong me or hurt me?

SENSITIVITY

"Therefore if you bring your gift to the altar, and there remember that your brother has something against you, leave your gift there before the altar, and go your way. First be reconciled to your brother, and then come and offer your gift" (Matthew 5:23–24).

1. Am I sensitive to the conviction and promptings of God's Spirit?
2. Am I quick to respond in humility and obedience to the conviction and promptings of God's Spirit?

EVANGELISM

"Then He said to them, 'Thus it is written, and thus it was necessary for the Christ to suffer and to rise from the dead the third day ... you are witnesses of these things'" (Luke 24:46, 48).

1. Do I have a burden for those who don't know Christ?
2. Do I consistently witness for Christ?

PRAYER

"Therefore I exhort first of all that supplications, prayers, intercessions, *and* giving of thanks be made for all men" (1 Timothy 2:1).

1. Am I faithful in praying for the needs of others?
2. Do I pray specifically, fervently, and faithfully for revival in my life, my church, and our nation?

REMEMBER:
YOU, IF NO ONE ELSE,
CAN BE A WALKING, JESUS-NOW REVIVAL!

Walking
in the Light
of God's
Word

**Let the peace of Christ rule in your hearts, to which indeed
you were called in one body; and be thankful. (Colossians 3:15 NASB)**

Claim the promise of His peace as you continue to explore a deepened journey in this Jesus-Now Awakening. Continue to experience this Scripture and be thankful for the wonder of His grace. Make this prayer your own!

"Blessed be the God and Father of our Lord Jesus Christ, who according to His great mercy has caused [me] to be born again to a living hope through the resurrection of Jesus Christ from the dead, to *obtain* an inheritance *which is* imperishable and undefiled and will not fade away, reserved in heaven for [me], who [is] protected by the power of God through faith for a salvation ready to be revealed in the last time. In this [I] greatly rejoice, even though now for a little while, if necessary, [I] have been distressed by various trials, so that the proof of [my] faith, being more precious than gold which is perishable, even though tested by fire, may be found to result in praise and glory and honor at the revelation of Jesus Christ; and though [I] have not seen Him, [I] love Him, and though [I] do not see Him now, but believe in Him, [I] greatly rejoice with joy inexpressible and full of glory" (1 Peter 1:3–8 NASB).

**M-6 Bearing witness of confident peace and expectant hope
in God's lordship in all things**

SPIRIT-
EMPOWERED
Faith

Resources

The following organizations and individuals mentioned in *Jesus Now* would be pleased to send you more information about their respective ministries in spiritual awakening, evangelism, and prayer.

Awakening America Alliance
awakeningamerica.us

Blackaby Ministries International (Henry Blackaby)
blackaby.net

Billy Graham Evangelistic Association
billygraham.org

Billy Graham Library
billygrahamlibrary.org

Billy Graham Training Center
thecove.org

Brooklyn Tabernacle
brooklyntabernacle.org

Campus Renewal
campusrenewal.org

Cannon Beach Conference Center
cbcc.net

Center for World Revival and Awakening
oneomc.org

Christ for all the Nations (Daniel Kolenda)
cfan.org

Converge
converge.org

CRU (Campus Crusade for Christ, International)
cru.org

Dare 2 Share Ministries
dare2share.org

Donica Hudson
donicahudson@gmail.com

Doug Small
Jesus.net

Global Media Outreach
globalmediaoutreach.com

Hollywood Prayer Network
Hollywoodprayernetwork.org

Kelly Green Global
kellygreenglobal.com

International Renewal Ministries
prayersummits.net

International Students Incorporated
isionline.org

Life Action Ministries
lifeaction.org

Mission America Coalition
missionamerica.org

National Day of Prayer
nationaldayofprayer.org
New York City Leadership Center (Mac Pier)
nycleadership.com

Proclaim HOPE!
proclaimhope.org

Promise Keepers
promisekeepers.org

PULSE Movement
pulsemovement.com

RESET
resetmovement.com

Revive Our Hearts (Nancy Leigh DeMoss)
reviveourhearts.com

See You at the Pole
syatp.org

World Revival Awakening (Dale Schlafer)
revivalandawakening.org

Corporate or Group Intercession

by Bill Eubank

Intercession is prayer that pleads with God for your needs and the needs of others. But it is also much more than that. Intercession involves taking hold of God's will and refusing to let go until His will comes to pass. Intercessory prayer is not the same as prayers for yourself, or for "enlightenment," or for spiritual gifts, or for guidance, or any personal matter, or any glittering generality. Intercession is not just praying for someone else's needs. Intercession is praying with the real hope and real intent that God would step in and act for the positive advancement of some specific other person or groups of people or community. It is trusting God to act, even if it's not in the manner or timing we seek. God wants us to ask, even *urgently*. It is casting our weakness before God's strength, and (at its best) having a bit of God's' passion burn in us.

If you are born again, you are God's son or daughter (John 1:12). As His child, you have a direct "hotline" to God. At any time, you can boldly come into His presence (Hebrews 4:16). This incredible access to God is the basis for intercession. Once you are in God's presence, you can now discover His battle plan for the situation you are facing. Because prayer alone is not enough—you need a target for your prayers!

To discover God's plan, all you have to do is *ask*. The Bible says, "If any of you lacks wisdom, let him ask of God, who gives to all liberally and without reproach, and it will be given to him" (James 1:5). When we ask God for wisdom, His desires will become the focus of our prayers. Let God change the way you think. Then you will know how to do everything that is good and pleasing to Him (Romans 12:2).

In preparation to coming into a time of intercession, each person should individually pray and ask the Holy Spirit what He would have us pray. Here is some suggested prayer etiquette when interceding in a group:

1. Our prayers should be short and focused on the area that the Spirit is leading. Listen carefully to what your fellow intercessors are praying to see if the Spirit would have you add to or build on their prayer.

2. As we pray short focused prayers, it is easier for others to join us in agreement or add their prayer for similar needs.

3. Encourage others by agreeing or saying amen in a quiet voice when someone prays something with which your spirit bears witness.

4. There will be times when the Spirit will show a person Scripture that relates with what is being prayed. They can share the Scripture and connect what the Spirit is showing them.

5. Do not be afraid of silence as you pray. Every moment does not have to be filled with words. Sometimes the Lord causes the group to be silent, so that people have the time to clearly hear what the Spirit is saying to their hearts.

6. Group intercession is corporate in nature. The Holy Spirit will lead as He wills. Therefore, each participant should seek to sense what the Spirit would have him/her pray at any given time to contribute to the whole.

7. You may have a burning desire to pray in a certain direction, but it is important that you wait before the Spirit to make sure that He would have you offer prayer from your "burning desire."

8. There are times when the Spirit is not leading in the direction that you thought He was. This is where maturity reveals that it is our responsibility to sincerely seek His guidance and direction.

9. If a participant begins to share his/her thoughts with the group instead of speaking to God, the leader or person with discernment should gently encourage everyone to focus on God and speak directly to Him.

10. There will be time after corporate intercession to share ideas, thoughts, and experiences with each other.

11. The great blessing of effective corporate intercession should be a sense that that group has "heard" or understood the direction of the Spirit for that time and feel that they prayed in that way.

About the Great Commandment Network

The Great Commandment Network is an international collaborative network of strategic kingdom leaders from the faith community, marketplace, education, and caregiving fields who prioritize the powerful simplicity of the words of Jesus to love God, love others, and see others become His followers (Matthew 22:37–40, Matthew 28:19–20).

THE GREAT COMMANDMENT NETWORK IS SERVED THROUGH THE FOLLOWING:

Relationship Press – This team collaborates, supports, and joins together with churches, denominational partners, and professional associates to develop, print, and produce resources that facilitate ongoing Great Commandment ministry.

The Center for Relational Leadership – Their mission is to teach, train, and mentor both ministry and corporate leaders in Great Commandment principles, seeking to equip leaders with relational skills so they might lead as Jesus led.

The Galatians 6:6 Retreat Ministry – This ministry offers a unique two-day retreat for ministers and their spouses for personal renewal and for reestablishing and affirming ministry and family priorities.

The Center for Relational Care (CRC) – The CRC provides therapy and support to relationships in crisis through an accelerated process of growth and healing, including Relational Care Intensives for couples, families, and singles.

For more information on how you, your church, ministry, denomination, or movement can be served by the Great Commandment Network write or call:

Great Commandment Network
2511 South Lakeline Blvd.
Cedar Park, Texas 78613
#800-881-8008
Or visit our website: www.GreatCommandment.net

A Spirit-Empowered Faith

**Expresses Itself in Great Commission Living
Empowered by Great Commandment Love**

**begins with the end in mind:
The Great Commission calls us
to make disciples.**

*"Go therefore and make disciples of all the nations, baptizing them in
the name of the Father and the Son and the Holy Spirit teaching them
to observe all things that I have commanded you; and lo, I am with
you always, even to the end of the age."* (Matthew 28:19–20)

The ultimate goal of our faith journey is to relate to the person of Jesus, because it is our relational connection to Jesus that will produce Christ-likeness and spiritual growth. This relational perspective of discipleship is required if we hope to have a faith that is marked by the Spirit's power.

Models of discipleship that are based solely upon what we *know* and what we *do* are incomplete, lacking the empowerment of a life of loving and living intimately with Jesus. **A Spirit-empowered faith is relational and impossible to realize apart from a special work of the Spirit.** For example, the Spirit-empowered outcome of "listening to and hearing God" implies relationship—it is both relational in focus and requires the Holy Spirit's power to live.

**begins at the right place:
The Great Commandment calls us to
start with loving God and loving others.**

*"'You shall love the Lord your God with all your heart, with all your soul,
and with all your mind.' This is the first and great commandment.
And the second is like it: 'You shall love your neighbor as yourself.'
On these two commandments hang all the Law and the Prophets."*
(Matthew 22:37–40)

Relevant discipleship does not begin with doctrines or teaching, parables or stewardship—but with loving the Lord with all your heart, mind, soul, and strength and then loving the people closest to you. Since Matthew 22:37–40 gives us the first and greatest commandment, *a Spirit-empowered faith starts where the Great Commandment tells us to start: A disciple must first learn to deeply love the Lord and to express His love to the "nearest ones"—his or her family, church, and community (and in that order).*

 embraces a relational process of Christlikeness.

Scripture reminds us that there are three sources of light for our journey: Jesus, His Word, and His people. The process of discipleship (or becoming more like Jesus) occurs as we relate intimately with each source of light.

"Walk while you have the light, lest darkness overtake you." (John 12:35)

Spirit-empowered discipleship will require a lifestyle of:
- Fresh encounters with Jesus (John 8:12)
- Frequent experiences of Scripture (Psalm 119:105)
- Faithful engagement with God's people (Matthew 5:14)

 can be defined with observable outcomes using a biblical framework.

The metrics for measuring Spirit-empowered faith or the growth of a disciple come from Scripture and are organized/framed around four distinct dimensions of a disciple who serves.

And He Himself gave some to be apostles, some prophets,
some evangelists, and some pastors and teachers,
for the equipping of the saints for the work of ministry,
for the edifying of the body of Christ.
(Ephesians 4:11–12)

A relational framework for organizing Spirit-Empowered Discipleship Outcomes draws from a cluster analysis of several Greek (*diakoneo, leitourgeo, douleuo*) and Hebrew words ('*abad, Sharat*), which elaborate on the Ephesians 4:12 declaration that Christ's followers are to be equipped for works of ministry or service. Therefore, the 40 Spirit-Empowered Faith Outcomes have been identified and organized around:

* Serving/loving the Lord – *While they were* **ministering** *to the Lord and fasting* (Acts 13:2 NASB).[1]

* Serving/loving the Word – *But we will devote ourselves to prayer and to the* **ministry** *of the word* (Acts 6:4 NASB).[2]

* Serving/loving people – *Through love* **serve** *one another* (Galatians 5:13 NASB).[3]

* Serving/loving His mission – *Now all these things are from God, who reconciled us to Himself through Christ and gave us the* **ministry** *of reconciliation* (2 Corinthians 5:18 NASB).[4]

---

1 Ferguson, David L. *Great Commandment Principle*. Cedar Park, Texas: Relationship Press, 2013.
2 Ferguson, David L. *Relational Foundations*. Cedar Park, Texas: Relationship Press, 2004.
3 Ferguson, David L. *Relational Discipleship*. Cedar Park, Texas: Relationship Press, 2005.
4 "Spirit Empowered Outcomes," www.empowered21.com, Empowered 21 Global Council, http://empowered21.com/discipleship-materials/.

A Spirit-Empowered Disciple

A SPIRIT-EMPOWERED DISCIPLE LOVES THE LORD THROUGH

L1. Practicing thanksgiving in all things
Enter into His gates with thanksgiving (Ps. 100:4). *In everything give thanks* (1 Th. 5:18). *As sorrowful, yet always rejoicing* (2 Cor. 6:10).

L2. Listening to and hearing God for direction and discernment
"Speak, Lord, for Your servant hears" (1 Sam. 3:8–9). *Mary, who also sat at Jesus' feet and heard His word* (Lk. 10:38–42). *And the Lord said, "Shall I hide from Abraham what I am doing … ?"* (Gen. 18:17). *But as the same anointing teaches you concerning all things …* (1 Jn. 2:27).

L3. Experiencing God as He really is through deepened intimacy with Him
"Hear, O Israel: The Lord our God, the Lord is one! You shall love the Lord your God with all your heart, with all your soul, and with all your strength" (Deut. 6:4–5). *Therefore the Lord will wait, that He may be gracious to you; and therefore He will be exalted, that He may have mercy on you. For the Lord is a God of justice …* (Is. 30:18). See also John 14:9.

L4. Rejoicing regularly in my identity as "His Beloved"
And his banner over me was love (Song of Sol. 2:4). *To the praise of the glory of His grace, by which He made us accepted in the Beloved* (Eph. 1:6). *For so He gives His beloved sleep* (Ps. 127:2).

L5. Living with a passionate longing for purity and to please Him in all things
Who may ascend into the hill of the Lord? … He who has clean hands and a pure heart (Ps. 24:3–4). *Beloved, let us cleanse ourselves from all filthiness of flesh and spirit, perfecting holiness in the fear of God* (2 Cor. 7:1). *"I always do those things that please Him"* (Jn. 8:29). *"Though He slay me, yet will I trust Him"* (Job 13:15).

L6. Consistent practice of self-denial, fasting, and solitude rest

He turned and said to Peter, "Get behind me, Satan! You are offense to Me, for you are not mindful of the things of God, but the things of men" (Mt. 16:23). *"But you, when you fast …"* (Mt. 6:17). *"Be still, and know that I am God"* (Ps. 46:10).

L7. Entering often into Spirit-led praise and worship

Bless the Lord, O my soul, and all that is within me (Ps. 103:1). *Serve the Lord with fear* (Ps. 2:11). *I thank You, Father, Lord of heaven and earth* (Mt. 11:25).

L8. Disciplined, bold, and believing prayer

Praying always with all prayer and supplication in the Spirit (Eph. 6:18). *"Call to Me, and I will answer you"* (Jer. 33:3). *If we ask anything according to His will, He hears us. And if we know that He hears us, whatever we ask, we know that we have the petitions that we have asked of Him* (1 Jn. 5:14–15).

L9. Yielding to the Spirit's fullness as life in the Spirit brings supernatural intimacy with the Lord, manifestation of divine gifts, and witness of the fruit of the Spirit

For by one Spirit we were all baptized into one body—whether Jews or Greeks, whether slaves or free—and have all been made to drink into one Spirit (1 Cor. 12:13). *"But you shall receive power when the Holy Spirit has come upon you"* (Acts 1:8). *But the manifestation of the Spirit is given to each one for the profit of all* (1 Cor. 12:7). See also 1 Pet. 4:10 and Rom. 12:6.

L10. Practicing the presence of the Lord, yielding to the Spirit's work of Christlikeness

But we all, with unveiled face, … are being transformed into the same from glory to glory, just as by the Spirit of the Lord (2 Cor. 3:18). *As the deer pants for the water brooks, so pants my soul after You, O God* (Ps. 42:1).

A SPIRIT-EMPOWERED DISCIPLE LOVES THE WORD THROUGH

W1. Frequently being led by the Spirit into deeper love for the One who wrote the Word

" 'You shall love the Lord your God ... .' 'You shall love neighbor as yourself.' On these two commandments hang all the Law and the Prophets" (Mt. 22:37–40). And I will delight myself in Your commandments, which I love. (Ps. 119:47). "The fear of the LORD is clean ... . More to be desired are they than gold ... sweeter also than honey" (Ps. 19:9–10).

W2. Being a "living epistle" in reverence and awe as His Word becomes real in my life, vocation, and calling

You are our epistle written in our hearts, known and read by all men (2 Cor. 3:2). And the Word became flesh and dwelt among us (Jn. 1:14). Husbands, love your wives ... cleanse her with the washing of water by the word (Eph. 5:25–26). See also Tit. 2:5. And whatever you do, do it heartily, as to the Lord and not to men (Col. 3:23).

W3. Yielding to the Scripture's protective cautions and transforming power to bring life change in me

Through Your precepts I get understanding; therefore I hate every false way (Ps. 119:104). "Let it be to me according to your word" (Lk. 1:38). How can a young man cleanse his way? By taking heed according to Your word (Ps. 119:9). See also Col. 3:16–17.

W4. Humbly and vulnerably sharing of the Spirit's transforming work through the Word

I will speak of your testimonies also before kings, and will not be ashamed (Ps. 119:46). Preach the word! Be ready in season and out of season (2 Tim. 4:2).

W5. Meditating consistently on more and more of the Word hidden in the heart

Your word I have hidden in my heart, that I might not sin against You (Ps. 119:11). *Let the words of my mouth and the meditation of my heart be acceptable in Your sight, O LORD, my strength and my Redeemer* (Ps. 19:14).

W6. Encountering Jesus in the Word for deepened transformation in Christlikeness

But we all, with unveiled face, … are being transformed into the same image from glory to glory, just as by the Spirit of the Lord (2 Cor. 3:18). *If you abide in Me, and My words abide in you, you will ask what you desire, and it shall be done for you* (Jn. 15:7). See also Lk. 24:32, Ps. 119:136, and 2 Cor. 1:20.

W7. A life explained as one of "experiencing Scripture"

But this is what was spoken by the prophet Joel (Acts 2:16). *This is my comfort in my affliction, for Your word has given me life* (Ps. 119:50). *My soul breaks with longing for Your judgements at all times* (Ps. 119:20).

W8. Living "naturally supernatural" in all of life as His Spirit makes the written Word (*logos*) the living Word (rhema)

*So then aith comes by hearing, and hearing by the word (*rhema*) of God* (Rom. 10:17). *Your word is a lamp to my feet and a light to my path* (Ps. 119:105).

W9. Living abundantly "in the present" as His Word brings healing to hurt and anger, guilt, fear, and condemnation—which are heart hindrances to life abundant

"The thief does not come except to steal, and to kill, and to destroy" (Jn. 10:10). *I will run the course of Your commandments, for You shall enlarge my heart* (Ps. 119:32). *"And you shall know the truth, and the truth shall make you free"* (Jn. 8:32). *Stand fast therefore in the liberty by which Christ has made us free, and do not be entangled again with a yoke of bondage* (Gal. 5:1).

W10. Implicit, unwavering trust that His Word will never fail
"The grass withers, the flower fades, but the word of our God stands forever" (Is. 40:8). *"So shall My word be that goes forth from My mouth; it shall not return to Me void"* (Is. 55:11).

A SPIRIT-EMPOWERED DISCIPLE LOVES PEOPLE THROUGH

P1. Living a Spirit-led life of doing good in all of life: relationships and vocation, community and calling
Who went about doing good ... (Acts 10:38). *"Let your light so shine before men, that they may see your good works and glorify your Father in heaven"* (Mt. 5:16). *"But love your enemies, do good, and lend, hoping for nothing in return; and your reward will be great, and you will be sons of the Most High. For He is kind to the unthankful and evil"* (Lk. 6:35). See also Rom. 15:2.

P2. "Startling people" with loving initiatives to "give first"
"Give, and it will be given to you: good measure, pressed down, shaken together, and running over will be put into your bosom" (Lk. 6:38). *Then Jesus said, "Father, forgive them, for they do not know what they do"* (Lk. 23:34). See also Lk. 23:43 and Jn. 19:27.

P3. Discerning the relational needs of others with a heart to give of His love
Let no corrupt word proceed out of your mouth, but what is good for necessary edification, that it might impart grace to the hearers (Eph. 4:29). *And my God shall supply all your need according to His riches in glory by Christ Jesus* (Phil. 4:19). See also Lk. 6:30.

P4. Seeing people as needing BOTH redemption from sin AND intimacy in relationships, addressing both human fallen-ness and aloneness
But God demonstrates His own love toward us, in that while we were still sinners, Christ died for us (Rom. 5:8). And when Jesus came to the place, He looked up and saw him, and said to him, "Zacchaeus, make haste and come down, for today I must stay at your house" (Lk. 19:5). See also Mk. 8:24 and Gen. 2:18.

P5. Ministering His life and love to our nearest ones at home and with family as well as faithful engagement in His body, the church
Husbands, likewise, dwell with them with understanding, giving honor to the wife, as to the weaker vessel, and as being heirs together of the grace of life, that your prayers may not be hindered (1 Pet. 3:7). See also 1 Pet. 3:1 and Ps. 127:3.

P6. Expressing the fruit of the Spirit as a lifestyle and identity
But the fruit of the Spirit is love, joy, peace, longsuffering, kindness, goodness, faithfulness, gentleness, self-control (Gal. 5:22–23). A man's stomach shall be satisfied from the fruit of his mouth; From the produce of his lips he shall be filled (Prov. 18:20).

P7. Expecting and demonstrating the supernatural as His spiritual gifts are made manifest and His grace is at work by His Spirit
In mighty signs and wonders, by the power of the Spirit of God, so that from Jerusalem and round about to Illyricum I have fully preached the gospel of Christ (Rom. 15:19). "Most assuredly, I say to you, he who believes in Me, the works that I do he will do also" (Jn. 14:12). See also 1 Cor. 14:1.

P8. Taking courageous initiative as a peacemaker, reconciling relationships along life's journey
Be at peace among yourselves (1 Th. 5:13). For He Himself is our peace, who has made both one, and has broken down the middle wall of separation (Eph. 2:14). Confess your trespasses to one another, and pray for one another, that you may be healed (Jas. 5:16).

P9. Demonstrating His love to an ever growing network of "others" as He continues to challenge us to love "beyond our comfort"
He who says, "I know Him," and does not keep His commandments, is a liar, and the truth is not in him (1 Jn. 2:4). If someone says, "I love God," and hates his brother, he is a liar; for he who does not love his brother whom he has seen, how can he love God whom he has not seen? (1 Jn. 4:20).

P10. Humbly acknowledging to the Lord, ourselves, and others that it is Jesus in and through us who is loving others at their point of need
"Take My yoke upon you and learn from Me, for I am gentle and lowly in heart, and you will find rest for your souls" (Mt. 11:29). "If I then, your Lord and Teacher, have washed your feet, you also ought to wash one another's feet" (Jn. 13:14).

A SPIRIT-EMPOWERED DISCIPLE LOVES HIS MISSION THROUGH

M1. Imparting the gospel and one's very life in daily activities and relationships, vocation and community
So, affectionately longing for you, we were well pleased to impart to you not only the gospel of God, but also our own lives, because you had become dear to us (1 Th. 2:8–9). See also Eph. 6:19.

M2. Expressing and extending the kingdom of God as compassion, |justice, love, and forgiveness are shared
"I must preach the kingdom of God to the other cities also, because for this purpose I have been sent" (Lk. 4:43). "As You sent Me into the world, I also have sent them into the world" (Jn. 17:18). Restore to me the joy of Your salvation, and uphold me by Your generous Spirit. Then I will teach transgressors Your ways, and sinners shall be converted to You (Ps. 51:12–13). See also Mic. 6:8.

M3. Championing Jesus as the only hope of eternal life and abundant living

"Nor is there salvation in any other, for there is no other name under heaven given among men by which we must be saved" (Acts 4:12). *"The thief does not come except to steal, and to kill, and to destroy. I have come so that they may have life, and that they have it more abundantly"* (Jn. 10:10). See also Acts 4:12 and Jn. 14:6.

M4. Yielding to the Spirit's role to convict others as He chooses, resisting expressions of condemnation

"And when He has come, He will convict the world of sin, and of righteousness, and of judgment" (Jn. 16:8). *Who is he who condemns? It is Christ who died, and furthermore is also risen, who is even at the right hand of God, who also makes intercession for us* (Rom. 8:34). See also Rom. 8:1.

M5. Ministering His life and love to the "least of these"

"Then He will answer them saying, 'Assuredly, I say to you inasmuch as you did not do it to one of the least of these, you did not do it to Me'" (Mt. 25:45). *Pure and undefiled religion before God and the Father is this: to visit orphans and widows in their trouble, and to keep oneself unspotted from the world* (Jas. 1:27).

M6. Bearing witness of a confident peace and expectant hope in God's lordship in all things

Now may the Lord of peace Himself give you peace always in every way. The Lord be with you all (2 Thess. 3:16). *And let the peace of God rule in your hearts, to which also you were called in one body; and be thankful* (Col. 3:15). See also Rom. 8:28 and Ps. 146:5.

M7. Faithfully sharing of time, talent, gifts, and resources in furthering His mission

Of which I became a minister according to the stewardship from God which was given to me for you, to fulfill the word of God (Col. 1:25). *"For everyone to whom much is given, from him much will be required"* (Lk. 12:48). See also 1 Cor. 4:1–2.

M8. **Attentive listening to others' story, vulnerably sharing of our story, and a sensitive witness of Jesus' story as life's ultimate hope; developing your story of prodigal, preoccupied and pain-filled living; listening for others' story and sharing Jesus' story**
But sanctify the Lord God in your hearts, and always be ready to give a defense to everyone who asks you a reason for the hope that is in you, with meekness and fear (1 Pet. 3:15). *"For this my son was dead and is alive again"* (Luke 15:24). See also Mk. 5:21–42 and Jn. 9:1–35.

M9. **Pouring our life into others, making disciples who in turn make disciples of others**
"Go therefore and make disciples of all the nations, baptizing them in the name of the Father and of the Son and of the Holy Spirit, teaching them to observe all things that I commanded you; and lo, I am with you always, even to the end of the age" (Mt. 28:19–20). See also 2 Tim. 2:2.

M10. **Living submissively within His body, the Church, as instruction and encouragement; reproof and correction are graciously received by faithful disciples**
Submitting to one another in the fear of God (Eph. 5:21). *Brethren, if a man is overtaken in any trespass, you who are spiritual restore such a one in a spirit of gentleness, considering yourself lest you also be tempted* (Gal. 6:1). See also Gal. 6:2.

ACKNOWLEDGMENTS

To write a book encouraging others to seek personal and national spiritual awakening is to learn the meaning of humility. The more I wrote about God's awesome power, the more I realized how inadequate I am on my own. So it was a blessing to work with Mark Cutshall. If this book is useful, clear, and vivid, it is because of Mark's tremendous literary gift. I'm so grateful for his help and for his friendship.

Dr. Lewis Drummond, the Billy Graham professor of evangelism at Beeson Divinity School and president emeritus of Southeastern Seminary, has been my spiritual mentor in the area of the Pietistic Movement, spiritual awakening, and evangelism. I'm thankful to Dr. Drummond for being the vessel that God has used to touch my life deeply regarding His plans for our world and for the future.

Dr. Charles Riggs, the director emeritus of counseling and follow-up for the Billy Graham Evangelistic Association, has been my spiritual Paul for twenty years. His challenge to my life relative to the Word of God and my walk in the Holy Spirit has exhorted and encouraged me to rest in the Lord for all that He could and would do through me. Also, thanks to Gene Warr and Jack Humphreys for being Barnabases in my spiritual life.

Kathy Maas, the production and communications team leader for International Students, Inc., has been a vital player in reviewing the manuscript, offering concise suggestions and correction, and personal encouragement.

My thanks also to those who have encouraged this work and reviewed the manuscript where necessary: Dr. David Ferguson,

Carlton Garborg, David Sluka, Terri Snead, Kay Horner, Pastor Dennis Gallaher, Wanda Bailey, Dr. Joe Aldrich, Dr. Bob Coleman, Dr. Tim Beougher, Carol Speirs, and the one who has been a major influence in all that God has done to prepare the church for this great movement of His Spirit that is just beginning—Dr. Billy Graham.

NOTES

Introduction

1 Raul Gonzales, in discussion with the author, 4 February 1994.

Chapter 1

1 Not her real name.

2 Tom Baker, in discussion with the author, 1 February 1994.

3 Richard Owen Roberts, *Revival* (Wheaton: Tyndale House Publishers, Inc., 1985), 6.

Chapter 2

1 Billy Graham, "A Fresh Vision for America," *Billy Graham Evangelic Association,* 2012, accessed 2016, http://billygraham.org/. story/a-fresh-vision-for-america/

2 "Who We Are," *Proclaim Hope*, accessed June 10, 2016, https://www. proclaimhope.org/about/who-we-are.

3 David Bryant, interview with Kathy Maas, September 21, 2011.

4 Mac Pier, interview with Kathy Maas, July 8, 2011.

Chapter 3

1 Nancy Leigh DeMoss, ed, *The Rebirth of America* (Niles, MI: Arthur S. DeMoss Foundation, 1986), 46.

2 Mary Stewart Relfe, *Cure of All Ills* (Montgomery: League of Prayer, 1988), 19.

3 Bethany Fellowship, *America's Great Revivals* (Minneapolis: Bethany Fellowship, Inc.), 10.

4 Ibid., 13.

5 Ibid., 14.

6 Christian Life, *America's Great Revivals* (Grand Rapids: Bethany House.), 24.

7 J. Edwin Orr, "The Role of Prayer in Spiritual Awakening," (Randolf Productions, Inc., 2006).

8 Ibid.

9 Ibid.

10 Mary Relfe, *Cure of All Ills* (Montgomery: League of Prayer, 1988), 27.

11 "Spiritual Awakenings in North America," *Christian History Institute* 8.23 (1989): 25.

12 Bethany Fellowship, *America's Great Revivals,* 41.

13 Ibid.

14 Relfe, *Cure of All Ills,* 34.

15 Ibid., 40–42.

16 Alvin Reid, "A Lone Man and United Prayer: Jeremiah Lanphier and the Prayer Revival," *The Alvin Reid Blog, Revival and Awakening,* 2014, http://alvinreid.com/?p=3513.

17 Bethany Fellowship, *America's Great Revivals,* 64.

18 Ibid., 76.

19 Ibid., 77.

20 Ibid., 60.

21 Charles G. Finney, *Lectures on Revival of Religion* (New York: Fleming H. Revell, 1988), 22–34.

22 "Franklin Graham: Praying for the Next Great Awakening," *Billy Graham Evangelic Association* (2014), accessed June 13, 2016, http://billygraham.org/story/franklin-graham-praying-for-the-next-great-awakening/.

23 "Billy Graham's Prayer for the Nation," accessed June 13, 2016, http://www.beliefnet.com/Prayers/Christian/Gratitude/Billy-Grahams-Prayer-For-The-Nation.aspx.

Chapter 4

1 Eryn Sun, "Jefferson Bethke 'Humbled' by Critique of His 'Why I Hate Religion, But Love Jesus' Video," *Christian Post* (2012), accessed June 13, 2016, http://www.christianpost.com/news/jefferson-bethke-humbled-by-critique-of-his-why-i-hate-religion-but-love-jesus-video-67308/.

2 Fanny Crosby, "I Am Thine, O Lord: Draw Me Nearer," *Hymn Time* (2015), accessed June 13, 2016, http://www.hymntime.com/tch/htm/i/a/t/iatolord.htm.

Chapter 5

1 Finney, *Lectures on Revival of Religion,* 22–34.

2 Joe Aldrich, in discussion with the author, February 8, 1994.

3 Ibid.

4 Ibid.

5   Ibid.

6   George Derksen, in discussion with the author, December 6, 1994.

7   Ibid.

8   James W. Tharp, letter, February 28, 1994.

9   Nell Barr, in discussion with the author, November 28, 1994.

10 Ibid.

11 Ibid.

12 Mac Pier, in discussion with the author, July 8, 2011.

13 Ibid.

14 Ibid.

15 Ibid.

16 Ibid.

17 "Mission Statement" (Wheaton: Concerts of Prayer International, 1994), 1.

18 Ibid.

19 Bill Bright, letter, October 7, 1994, 2.

20 Ibid.

21 Steve Hallin discussion with the author, December 7, 1994.

22 Chris McFarland, in discussion with the author, November 17, 2014.

23 Karen Covell, in discussion with the author, February 24, 2015.

24 Bill Eubank, in discussion with the author, November 13, 2014.

25 Ibid.

26 Bruce Snell, in discussion with the author, June 17, 2014.

27 Colin C. Whittaker, *Great Revivals* (Springfield: Gospel Publishing House, 1984), 181–83.

Chapter 6

1   Lewis Drummond, in discussion with the author, December 19, 1994.

2   "The Search for the Sacred: America's Quest for Spiritual Meaning," *Newsweek*, November 28, 1994.

3   Lewis Drummond, in discussion with the author, December 19, 1994.

4   *Newsweek*, 53–62.

5   Lewis Drummond in discussion with the author, January 4, 1995.

6   Ibid.

7   Ibid.

Chapter 7

1   *National & International Religion Report*, December 26, 1994: 1.

2   Ibid.

3   Wayne Atcheson, Billy Graham Library, May 18, 2016.

4   James Burns, *The Laws of Revival* (Minneapolis: World Wide Publications, 1993), 13.

5   James Burns, *Revivals, Their Laws and Leaders* (Grand Rapids: Baker, 1960), 28.

6   Bertha Smith, *Go Home and Tell* (Nashville: Broadman Press, 1965).

7   Burns, *The Laws of Revival*, 43.

8   David Franklin, in discussion with the author, February 18, 2015.

9   Ibid.

Chapter 8

1   *National & International Religion Report*, December 26, 1994: 1.

2   Ibid.

3   Ibid.

4   Ibid.

5   David McKenna, in discussion with the author, January 10, 1995.

6   Kristy Etheridge, "A Hug, a Prayer and a Wedding: Stories from Chaplains in Ferguson," *Billy Graham Evangelistic Association* (2014), accessed April 28, 2015.

7   Barbara Kantrowitz, "In Search of the Sacred," *Newsweek* (1994): 55.

8   Ibid.

9   Nancy Leigh DeMoss, address to "A Special Call to Prayer & Fasting for Our Country," Orlando, Florida, December 7, 1994.

10 Bob Norsworthy, online computer correspondence, November 1, 1994.

ABOUT THE AUTHOR

Tom Phillips is a farm boy from Mississippi whose grandfather was a circuit-riding preacher. His family's spiritual heritage originated in the great awakenings throughout the Southeast, beginning in Kentucky, in the early 1800s. The Word of God as a daily guide for faith and practice bred a strong devotional life, a life of sharing God's love through Jesus, and the joy in the Lord that historically changed the southeastern portion of the United States and eventually touched Tom's family.

Tom Phillips' upbringing compelled him to share his faith as a young man. Desiring to help people, he began studying medicine with the intention of becoming a surgeon. But God intervened, calling him to share not physical healing but spiritual healing—the Good News of Jesus Christ, a loving and forgiving Lord and Savior. Tom's education quickly moved from medical school to seminary.

Tom yielded to God's call to a life of evangelism while in his second year of seminary. He realized the world had a desperate spiritual need and that a revived church could be the catalyst to renew society as had happened in previous revivals. God impressed upon Tom that he would share in a great revival to bring this nation back to Jesus' love and forgiveness. God's call opened to him a world of ministry, and eventually, the opportunity to serve with Billy Graham, where he saw millions surrender to salvation through Jesus.

To contact Tom Phillips, go to
TheCenterForAwakening.com